TALKERS, WATCHERS,
AND DOERS

TALKERS, WATCHERS, AND DOERS

Unlocking Your Child's Unique Learning Style

School Savvy Kids Series

Cheri Fuller

OUR GUARANTEE TO YOU

We believe so strongly in the message of our books that we are making this quality guarantee to you. If for any reason you are disappointed with the content of this book, return the title page to us with your name and address and we will refund to you the list price of the book. To help us serve you better, please briefly describe why you were disappointed. Mail your refund request to: Piñon Press, P.O. Box 35002, Colorado Springs, CO 80935.

ISBN 1-57683-599-5

Cover photo by Photodisc and Corbis
Cover design by David Carlson Design
Creative Team: Rachelle Gardner, Arvid Wallen, Darla Hightower, Glynese Northam

Publised in association with the literary agency of Alive Communications, Inc. 7680 Goddard Street, Suite 200, Colorado Springs, Colorado, 80920.

Content was originally included in *Unlocking Your Child's Learning Potential: How to Equip Kids to Succeed in School and Life* by Cheri Fuller, NavPress, 1994.

Some of the anecdotal illustrations in this book are true to life and are included with the permission of the persons involved. All other illustrations are composites of real situations, and any resemblance to people living or dead is coincidental.

Published in association with the literary agency of Alive Communications, Inc., 7680 Goddard Street, Suite 200, Colorado Springs, Colorado, 80920.

Fuller, Cheri.
  Talkers, watchers, and doers : unlocking your child's unique learning style / Cheri Fuller.
      p. cm. -- (School savvy kids)
  Includes bibliographical references.
  ISBN 1-57683-599-5
  1. Learning. 2. Cognitive styles in children. 3. Education--Parent participation. I. Title.
II. Series.

  LB1060.F84 2004
  370.15'23--dc22

                              2004006259

Printed in Canada
2 3 4 5 6 7 8 9 10 11 / 08 07 06 05

To my granddaughter Josephine Bryce Fuller

contents

acknowledgments

Special thanks to people who shared their experience, expertise, and encouragement with me: Karen DeClouet, Dr. Tim Campbell, Jerri Bell, Kaye Johns, Bitsy Thomas, Jane Henderson, Linda Swales, Jane Neidenfeuhr, Marilyn Morgan, Melanie Hemry, Lynn Fuller, Karen Gale, Kathy Veegeteveen, Bodie Thoene, Dr. John Sabolich, and many other parents and teachers who shared their insights about their own and their children's learning styles.

I am grateful to my editor Rachelle Gardner for all the insight and creativity she brought to this project, and also Liz Heaney, Traci Mullins, and the NavPress staff for helping to make this book a valuable resource for parents.

Special love and thanks to my husband, Holmes, and our three children, Justin, Christopher, and Alison, their spouses, and our lively grandchildren who keep me in the learning curve for life. And to friends and family who cared, prayed, and supported my work, my heartfelt thanks!

no two children learn alike

Karen was an active, energetic child. She rode her bike earlier than other kids in the neighborhood and was on the go all the time. Curious about everything, she learned best by doing "real-life" activities with her parents in the kitchen or manipulating things such as blocks.

Karen loved preschool, especially making animals out of clay, finger painting, and outdoor play. But when she was four years old and the letters of the alphabet were introduced, she had a hard time distinguishing between P and D, W and M, and other letters. The letters just didn't connect with the sounds.

Luckily Karen's mom, Gretchen, realized her daughter learned in a hands-on way, so she made two-foot-tall shapes of all the alphabet letters out of brightly colored material. Karen played with the stuffed letters, manipulated them, and turned them around different ways on the floor. Before long, she learned the alphabet letters and sounds, and was putting her big stuffed letters together to make simple words.

Karen's parents understood how their daughter learned best, and when she didn't seem to understand something, instead of saying, "Why aren't you paying attention; how could you be so stupid?" they thought, *How are you thinking about this, Karen?*

Thus, they gave their little "Doer" many opportunities for hands-on learning in her early years, which helped her master the basics and reinforced what she learned at school. She learned math best by handling concrete objects around the house. She learned about counting and measurements by helping her mom cook.

Even though at first reading was difficult for her, Karen's parents (who were avid readers themselves) read to her a great deal. They found books that were action-packed and in her areas of interest, and Karen became an excellent reader and writer. By age ten, she started writing her first novel on her computer and had ideas for ten different novels.

Like many active, hands-on learners, Karen didn't notice if her clothes matched—she was too busy with projects, the computer, or taking long bike rides. Very involved in athletics, she earned letters in four sports at school each year, and had plenty of energy for other activities.

Although "Doers" like Karen may be very bright, they're the most at-risk group for school failure and problems because school is mostly letters and numbers, abstract symbols on worksheets or books that can be hard to figure out. These kids make up the major population in "resource rooms" for learning disabled. But if their parents help them learn in ways that capitalize on their strengths, they can succeed.

Just as your child has a unique temperament and personality bent, she also has particular patterns for learning. Each child's brain is wired differently and many factors make up a person's learning style. Psychologists have long known there are distinct personality types. Wouldn't it be boring if we were all the same? Those differences in preferences, choices of hobbies and clothing, keep our families and our world exciting and interesting.

Just as kids have different personalities and physical traits, a number of factors affect kids' learning. They might learn best independently or a study group might be more effective for them. They may excel in a structured classroom with an adult teaching or they might prefer to discover concepts themselves through reading. Some students need to see the big picture before breaking down a concept into parts, and some learn best in logical steps and want rules for doing new tasks. Some learn best in a quiet room, and others need some background noise.[1]

Among the factors of learning style, one that plays a vital role in school performance is *how your child processes information.*

- Some kids learn best by seeing—reading, observing, looking at pictures and diagrams—that is, by visual learning. (We'll use the term "Watchers.")

- Some children's strength is hearing explanations and talking about the information—that is, by auditory learning. ("Talkers")

- Other kids, like Karen, need to get their muscles, movement, and/or touch involved in learning—by doing an experiment, rehearsing, or taking an active approach—that is, by kinesthetic learning. ("Doers")

- Many children use a combination of these three methods to understand and learn.

While most of us learn in all three ways at some point, scientists have discovered that in most children, one sense is more finely tuned and effective for learning than the others. We can compare the learner to a television set that can receive information on several different channels. Let's say you're at a lake cabin without cable service or a satellite dish. One channel usually comes in more clearly than the others. And just as you would tend to watch that stronger, clearer channel as the main source of your news and entertainment, the learner tends to rely on one means—the auditory, visual, or kinesthetic—as the primary way of receiving and processing information, and of expressing knowledge and ideas.[2]

If one station has constant interference and is blocked from effective use and the student doesn't know how to change channels, he's frustrated and may develop problems in the classroom.

Helen Keller's visual and auditory channels were not available for processing information or learning words. But when her sense of touch—her strength—was accessed to get through to her brain, the lightbulb went on and she understood language. Her brilliant mind was released to achieve and impact the world as she grew into adulthood. If we discover children's strengths, their mental growth can be enhanced and they can be more successful in school and life.

Discovering children's learning styles is not a panacea for

all learning problems, but even students who have been labeled "learning disabled" can compensate for their weaknesses and achieve more when we discover and use their skills and talents.[3]

As you look at different factors in this book, you'll discover your child's learning patterns—not to label or pigeonhole her as only one kind of learner, but to discover how the combination of her strengths and gifts and the particular way her brain is wired can be utilized to learn most effectively. Kids achieve more when they're understood by parents and teachers who show them ways to capitalize on their strengths and help them compensate for their weaknesses, so they aren't consistently overwhelmed or defeated.

the benefits

Whether you're a parent who has children in a public or private school or a homeschool mom with four kids at different grades, understanding their learning patterns can be invaluable. Teaching our children *how to learn* is as important as teaching them what to learn.

Here are some of the benefits:

- They concentrate better, retain more, and make higher grades.[4]

- They acquire a more positive view of learning, because kids' early learning experience, whether a string of successes or failures, strongly influences their motivation and view of themselves as learners.

- They become more active, independent learners. They "learn how to learn" and maximize the study time they have at home or school.

- They can learn to adapt to different teaching styles in the classroom.

- When they hit a snag, or are "stuck" in a subject or task that is difficult, they have tools to draw on to get over the obstacles and learn what they need to.

- Conflict over chores and homework between parents and children can be eliminated, resulting in more family harmony.

You see, children in the same family rarely learn the same way. Husbands and wives usually have distinct learning styles, and parents often approach tasks in different ways from their children, which can cause conflict. (That's why in a later chapter we'll look at your learning style as a parent.) The parent whose main learning channel is auditory may interpret a Doer's style as misbehavior. The visual parent may say, "Be quiet!" to her auditory learner, blocking the best means of study for the child who needs to say and hear the information to understand and remember it.

getting the most from this book

As you read the pages ahead, you'll discover new things about how you learn and how your kids learn. Instead of expecting them to learn just like you do, you can begin to talk about learning preferences. If your child could choose to practice math facts or vocabulary words in any way possible, how would he do it? You can read the chapter about parents' learning styles to get a better picture of how you learn best. And the descriptions of children and surveys in chapter 3 will help you gain a picture of your child's learning patterns.

Next, I encourage you to try some of the learning-style strategies suggested throughout the pages that follow and see which methods—or combinations of methods—help your child learn and remember important information. There are also lots of ideas for enhancing preschoolers' visual, auditory, and kinesthetic skills before they're ever in a classroom situation. Be sure to take "another look at smart" and discover ways to identify and develop your child's gifts and intelligence in chapters 8 and 9. Chapter 10 will give you suggestions on working with teachers without alienating them and ways to bypass kids' weaknesses. Be sure to read chapter 11 to your child so he can be inspired by the stories of learning-different people who struggled in school but achieved amazing things as adults.

I think you'll find, as I have, that when parents understand their children's strengths and show them how to capitalize on them, kids can excel. D and F struggles can be turned into A and B successes, confidence grows, and children become active learners with a pattern of achievement at school.

identifying your child's learning style

Did you know that the word *teacher* means "one who brings out the best in the student"? As parents, we are our children's first and best teachers. The more we know our kids, the more we can help them have successful learning experiences and develop and use their strengths. As a parent, you are actually better equipped than a teacher—with twenty or more students in a classroom—to discover this valuable information about your child, and to notice how the child tackles a problem and what method of study he turns to when under stress or time pressure.

Although individual studies support teaching to learning styles in the classroom, some educators feel there's not enough consistent evidence to justify it. However, there *is* extensive research on the advantages of helping kids learn to use cognitive strategies, or learning methods, that tap into their strengths. Over and over we've seen that students who know how they process information and use corresponding strategies do best and achieve the most in school and beyond.

Your child's learning style, which is as individual as her fingerprint, reflects her development, aptitudes, strengths, and weaknesses. Remember that there is no right or wrong learning style. It's just another way that people are different. Let's look at three basic areas that will help you as a parent identify and understand how your child learns best.

clues to learning strengths

Think back to the last time you took your child to a mall. Did she wander off gazing at things that caught her eye? Is she captivated by all the colorful sights? She may be a Watcher. (As a grown-up, this visually oriented person may go to the grocery store for several items, get sidetracked looking at things, and come home an hour and a half later.)

If you panicked because you couldn't find your child, did you discover her touching and feeling the merchandise—much to the salesperson's dismay—and twirling the racks around, opening doors, and climbing on furniture in the dressing room? In a toy store these Doers need to be supervised because if left to their own devices, they may take apart a game or toy to see how it works.

If your verbal child gets lost, you may find her chatting with another child, making friends with a salesperson, or talking someone out of a quarter for candy from the machine. Not liking to be alone, the Talker will usually look for someone to play or interact with.

how learners grow

As Donna, a mother of three, said, "I watch my just-turned three-year-old and know he will be a strong auditory learner. From a young age, he was proficient with his descriptions of events and objects. And although he is the youngest, he's the first one to respond to my verbal requests." When observed carefully, even infants show a bent or preference for one style or another. My visual baby Chris could be entertained by watching his colorful mobile or a bird outside the window. My most auditory child, Justin, was an early talker and responded best to my voice or music if he was upset. Our daughter Alison was a blend—she loved visual and auditory stimulation, especially music.

Yet as babies grow mentally, physically, and emotionally, their learning styles are also developing. From infancy to kindergarten and first grade, children tend to learn with a hands-on approach—by touching, feeling, crawling, and emptying out your kitchen drawer. That's why one of the most successful preschool programs, developed by Maria Montessori, was built on children's natural strengths with manipulatives, concrete materials, and direct experience.

By first or second grade, children's visual skills are developing, which is why reading instruction is begun at that age. The visual skills are not totally developed until fourth grade. And some children are what we call "late bloomers"—their visual skills may be delayed, which could cause difficulty in learning to read.

By fifth or sixth grade (and later for some children), the auditory or listening skills become stronger. That's why a teacher of sixth graders might give a thirty-minute presentation on the causes of the Civil War and expect the students to take notes, whereas if a kindergarten teacher primarily used lectures to teach, we'd wonder about her understanding of children. But just because some kids may be delayed in developing kinesthetically, auditorily, or visually, that doesn't mean they won't develop those skills.

"Children's brains start out immature," says Dr. Larry Silver, clinical professor of psychiatry at the Georgetown University School of Medicine. "Maturational spurts occur once or twice a year. It's as if a new computer chip enters in. And when that chip starts firing, there may be changes in the way a child learns."[1] Children are always learning, always developing. That's the good news—it's never too late to begin to help them learn more effectively.

visual learning: luke

Luke, a child with visual strengths, is a perceptive Watcher who processes and remembers information best by picturing something in his mind's eye and maintaining a mental image of it. This child has such a good visual memory, it's as if he has a copy machine in his brain, which will come in handy later in the classroom for spelling words and studying for tests.

As a little child, Luke was fascinated by his visual surroundings. An astute observer during family car trips, toddler Luke loved looking at the passing billboards on the highway, and often noticed things his older siblings and parents missed. He learned his colors early, and preferred playing with puzzles, drawing with crayons and markers, and watching television to other activities. He was a child of few words who communicated his feelings more with facial expressions and pictures he drew.

Luke, like many visually talented children, has a great imagination and loves to draw, so much so that his first-grade teacher—who did a lot of oral work, talking and explaining—wrote on his report card that he was a "daydreamer" who could get more done if he stayed on task. If there's no outline or visual thing to look at when the teacher talks for an extended time, he tunes out and finds something outside the window to gaze at, or he doodles.

Luke gets his homework done fastest at a neat, orderly desk (he doesn't like a lot of visual distraction) and likes to have his assignments written down. He can then be efficient at working alone. He often closes his eyes or looks at the ceiling when he is memorizing or recalling information he is tested on. He depends on seeing information—in print or on graphs, diagrams, and pictures—to learn. A good test-taker, Luke shines in math, where he can easily compute answers in his head.

One night Luke's mom came into his bedroom to say good night and check on him. The lights were out. He lay in his bed, looking happy and busy, but with nothing to do, at least that's how it appeared. She asked him what he was doing.

"When I can't sleep, I work the longest, most difficult math problems I can in my mind, draw the lines, write the signs, and figure them out. Then I can relax," he answered. How much better than counting sheep!

Your child may also be a strong visual learner if she:

☐ uses picture clues to give her meaning when reading a book

☐ does chores better when given a list of things to do on paper or written instructions

- ☐ remembers faces and forgets names
- ☐ notices details such as a new picture or object in the room, his mom's new haircut, or a change in the classroom bulletin board before anyone else
- ☐ learns fastest and understands best if you show her and allow her to see how things are put together or how they work
- ☐ watches others when in a social group instead of jumping into the action

auditory learning: amy

Amy, a child with auditory strengths, is a good listener, but what she really likes to do is talk. Amy has a mind like a tape recorder. She remembers what you said long after you said it, and then reminds you. Although more girls than boys have auditory and verbal strengths, like me you may have a son who is verbally talented.

From an early age, Amy talked in sentences and had a colorful vocabulary. In fact, although her mother loved to hear her stories and songs, sometimes she got tired of Amy's incessant chatter and needed a quiet break. Her speech sounded like a little adult's as she related made-up stories and riddles to her family.

Even as a preschooler, she took charge and directed her friends in "let's pretend" play. She was vocal about her feelings and a bit dramatic. If she drew a picture, she wanted to talk about her artwork. Her favorite part of kindergarten was show-and-tell, when she could share about a new pet or happening in her family.

In the classroom, Amy is called the teacher's pet by other kids because she gets called on so often. She follows oral directions easily and is quick to answer the teacher's questions. But she doesn't feel like the teacher's pet when she gets in trouble for talking too much during seatwork time. She spells everything like it sounds, so her words were sometimes written incorrectly until she started using a tape recorder to study her spelling words by hearing them. She also has trouble remembering multiplication tables, which slows her down during math tests. But Amy shines in creative writing and class discussions. Like most kids with auditory strengths, she moves her lips or whispers while trying to memorize facts or spelling words for a test. She verbalizes everything and needs to hear information and then say it in order to learn it.

In addition to the above, your child may be a strong auditory learner if she:

☐ is able to follow directions after listening to you once, and doesn't need things repeated

☐ likes listening to music tapes, the radio, singing, and hearing books read aloud

☐ remembers a telephone number, zip code, or name by repeating it a few times

☐ can maintain her focus just by listening in a class lecture or presentation, without having to be actively involved

☐ benefits from a phonics approach to learning to read

☐ solves problems by talking

kinesthetic or active learning: jamie

Jamie, a fifth grader, was burned out on schoolwork and considered by his teachers and parents to be an underachiever. He learned best by a hands-on approach but school was a lot of pencil-and-paper tasks. He was a star on the sports field, but fidgeted in the classroom. His dad, a quiet (and visually oriented) accountant, expected Jamie to be quiet when he studied and exerted pressure to get better performance. He even grounded his son when Jamie's grades weren't high enough or when he "played around" and moved instead of sitting still to study. Evening homework times became a war zone.

For kids like Jamie, "being still" requires so much mental energy that they can't concentrate on their work. He needs an active approach.

When Jamie had a lot of facts to learn for the Geography Bowl, I suggested his mom let him use his muscles in the practice sessions. While Meredith fired off the questions from the couch, Jamie bounced his Nerf basketball and shot a basket with each answer. "Something happened while he was active," his mom said. "He got a better imprint somehow on his memory. It also helped his focus and concentration." After their daily basketball/ geography sessions, Jamie won the right to represent his grade in the schoolwide Geography Bowl. And although he was the youngest student in the finals, competing against even eighth graders, he placed third—his first scholastic recognition ever. Using this approach, a whiteboard to practice vocabulary and spelling words, and some other strategies that used his strengths, he became one of the top students in his grade.

In addition to developing a more positive attitude toward his homework and himself as a learner, Jamie felt more affirmed by his dad. Some of the stress was removed from their relationship. Pleased with Jamie's achievement, Dad spent less time criticizing and more time supporting his son's active, hands-on approach to learning.

Your child may be a hands-on learner if he:

- [ ] remembers best what was done rather than what he was told, read, or talked to about
- [ ] seems to learn everything by experience, trial and error
- [ ] tries things out and always seems to be touching things, even if they are "off-limits"
- [ ] needs a lot of physical contact with parents, children, and teachers, and if he doesn't get the positive affection—hugs, pats, and so on—will nudge, push, and pinch other class-mates or siblings
- [ ] is so active that shoelaces become untied and shirttails pulled out seconds after he has been neatly dressed for the day

blends and combination learners

Some kids—about 30 percent—operate out of a blend of two or three strengths. As a preschooler, Jacob often asked to "see things" when his mother tried to explain something to him. He often played dress-up with costumes: He put his Batman costume over an elf costume, which was placed over his Frosty the

Snowman costume. He was also the one in the family who would first see a jet far off in the sky or find a lost object in the grass.

Yet even as a baby, Jacob was on the move. He was so energetic he almost wore his parents out, broke things from trying them out, and ran away from them at every juncture—at the park, mall, or church. He always loved to work and do "big jobs" at home. He wanted to learn how to wash clothes, so his mom taught him. By age six, he could wash, dry, and fold whites, darks, delicates, and towels with ease. In addition to his need to have his clothes match "just right," Jacob enjoyed this activity so much because it met his need to be doing something busy and productive.

As a preschooler, Jacob was most interested in the nursery rhymes his mom read when he could act them out. He learned them best by pretending to be Jack "jumping over the candlestick" or Humpty Dumpty "falling off the wall."

While Jacob had excellent teachers who taught him phonics, he still learned to read primarily by sight. Once he saw a word, he usually could remember it the next time. He began reading as a kindergartner, which was a little ahead of schedule in light of a slight developmental language delay. And when he couldn't depend on his sight-word vocabulary, he had good phonics skills to rely on.

By the time he was in the second grade, Jacob was excelling, partly because his parents understood his visual/kinesthetic strengths.

combining study strategies

Whether your child is strong in looking, listening, or watching, or in a combination, in the chapters that follow you will discover some strategies that will capitalize on her strengths and enable her to learn more in the classroom and at home. If she has a mixture of strengths, combine methods from the different chapters and you'll find her more motivated and engaged in learning.

discovering your own
learning style

One day a dad took his teenage son out to teach him to sail. He quickly reeled off a list of instructions of how to set the sails, and then told his son to do what he had said. His son tried but could remember only two steps. Dad again repeated the instructions, this time a little louder, but his son wasn't able to complete the task. Dad got so exasperated, he threw his son overboard into the water. So much for a fun day of sailing. It took until the boy was a senior in high school before their relationship was healed.

What this father didn't understand was how his way of processing information was different from his son's. A little understanding of his own learning style would have made a big difference. The more you are aware of yourself and the way you learn, the more you can understand and help your child. As parents, we tend to expect our children to learn things the way we do. Sometimes we even want our child to match our area of strength and be a "chip off the old block."

For example, Peggy became frustrated with Eric when she told him to clean up his room, bring in his skates and soccer ball, organize his baseball cards and toys, and take out the trash. After two hours, he hadn't completed any of it. Another mom, Joanna, couldn't understand why her daughter Holly didn't enjoy writing assignments the way she had in school. In fact, it puzzled her that Holly didn't like school at all. Frustrated dad Jack was weary of explaining fractions to his son Jeremy for the sixth time, and still Jeremy didn't understand them.

Expecting our kids to learn as we do can cause us to:

- Be frustrated if she doesn't understand or "get it" the way we explain a problem—this causes a lot of homework conflict and stress.

- Limit our child's learning and even bore her by not allowing for differences, not varying the activities and ways of presenting information (which can produce big problems for homeschooling parents who teach every subject every day).

- Be disappointed if our child with a different learning style doesn't achieve in the classroom. If he doesn't do well in a subject we excelled in with ease, we may think our child is lazy, stupid, or just not trying.

- Interpret the child's different learning style as misbehavior, a lack of listening, or even rebellion.

When Brad studied, he usually ended up pacing around the dining room with his flash cards while saying his multiplication tables. To his mom, this seemed the most natural way for him to practice for tests, and she allowed it. However, when Dad got home in the evening, he complained that Brad was making noise and playing around instead of studying. If he'd really concentrate and study as his big sister does, he'd excel too, Dad thought. Just as it was for this family, it's vital for you to understand your learning strengths and your child's in order to help and not hinder your child's learning.

siblings learn differently

First it's important to realize that rarely do all kids in the same family have the same way of processing information, unless they're identical twins. Fifteen-year-old identical twins Jennifer and Jessica are strongest visually: Seeing and reading is their favorite way to learn things. But they're also both Talkers (secondary strength) who like to study alone first and then ask each other questions. They excel in the same subjects—English, geography, and history—and receive generally the same grades on their report cards. Both play the piano, and neither are strong in sports or highly coordinated physically.

Sarah and Joanna are two-year-old fraternal twins. Sarah is very relational and nurturing. Her favorite activity is playing with dolls. Joanna is mechanically oriented, changing the dials on the VCR and stereo, building towers, and sorting shapes. Sarah is more advanced in language and was more content as a baby, whereas Joanna is more curious, active, and on the go.

In the Olsen family, Wynter, thirteen years old, is a Watcher. Although she's a versatile learner, her preference is visual. When she studies electricity, she wants to read all she can about it, do work sheets, and take the test. She excels in learning in this way. She's not interested in experiments and manipulatives because, in her own words, "They take too much time."

The Olsens' ten-year-old son, Chase, however, is a Doer—action is his middle name. When they read aloud the first few pages about electricity in their homeschool, he couldn't wait to get the wires and equipment his mom had gathered and do the experiment. Chase can fix almost anything. He also finds complex diagrams to assemble model airplanes easy, which shows spatial strengths. On his own, Chase has created a burglar alarm system, a radio, and a bell. But just reading about something leaves him cold. Chase and Wynter's mom is a Talker who likes to do a lot of explaining, but as she's understood her own and her kids' different learning styles, she finds they're more motivated about school.

opposites attract

Psychologists tell us that while we may feel comfortable with people like ourselves, we don't tend to marry them![1] Opposites do attract, and husbands and wives tend to have different learning styles. For example, being more auditory in my learning style, I think primarily in words, whereas my husband, Holmes, a visual/spatial learner, thinks in pictures. And I'm always amazed by the things he can picture! A whole house before he ever builds it, including all the interior detail, or even a whole neighborhood and how it could look after he developed it.

I think through many ideas at once and am happy juggling several projects at one time. Holmes thinks through one idea at a time, proceeding step by step, and does things in the proper order. I'm a "big picture" person, whereas he is a "detail" person. He operates in files; I use piles. (They need to be visible because what's out of sight is out of mind for me.)

If my success in school had depended on my visual and spatial skills, which are needed for proficiency in sewing and assembling things from directions, I would have spent a large amount of my day in the "resource room" for disabled learners. When I took up sewing, I spent hours trying to assemble and sew dresses for our daughter and ended up redoing sleeves and bodices three or more times and resorting to asking one of my visually talented friends or husband to help me through the complex parts.

Fortunately for me, school involved a lot of oral instruction and writing, which I enjoyed, and I was blessed with teachers who explained a lot. When reading, I tended to subvocalize, or say the words in my head. I talked through math story problems and was fortunate to have algebra and higher-math teachers who were expert explainers.

Although many kids have to do things at school all day that focus on their weaknesses, as adults we don't have to. Instead, we choose jobs that enable us to function in our area of strength. We tend to avoid our weakest areas and pick careers in which we have some success and interest.

Almost all radio broadcasters I have met are auditory/verbal learners (Talkers). This kind of learner might go into sales, become a manager, lawyer, secondary school teacher, secretary, speaker, or writer. They find jobs that require verbal input and interaction with other people. People with kinesthetic strengths are attracted to jobs where they move about rather than being stuck at a desk all day. Thus they become dentists, mechanics, actors, coaches, artists, builders, hairstylists, race car drivers, and surgeons. If they become teachers, they tend to choose kindergarten teaching or a subject like drama or science. People with visual strengths may be teachers, computer programmers and analysts, accountants, interior designers, stockbrokers, or artists. So first, think about your career or job, and how it reveals your strengths.

remembering a number

Somebody tells you a phone number, and you don't have any way to write it down so you have to remember it. Think about what goes through your mind as you try to memorize it. Do you say it out loud or repeat it several times in your mind? This is common for Talkers. Does your mind's eye "see" the number written in your address book? You might be a Watcher. Do you move your finger over an imaginary touch pad of the phone? This tactile way of processing information is common to Doers.

finding your way

How do you find your way around in a new city or someplace you've never been before? Directionality, or how you get your bearings and navigate in new surroundings, is another clue to how you learn best, easiest, and fastest.

We had just moved to Yarmouth, Maine, twenty miles north of Portland, and I had to go to downtown Portland occasionally to pick up Holmes or take one of the children for a doctor's appointment. I'd never driven in this city, so I knew I was in for a challenge. So how did I find my way? How would you find your way to a new place? And what do you do if you get lost?

The parent with auditory strengths like me needs clearly written directions telling in words how to get to the destination. If I get lost, I prefer to stop and ask someone for directions and write it down. In fact, I enjoy talking with folks along the way; I always learn something new or interesting. Occasionally this has backfired when the person I asked was just as much a newcomer as I was.

The visual person likes to use maps to find out how to get somewhere. My husband is a great map reader. But if he's been somewhere once, he remembers all the landmarks and doesn't need a map. And if he gets lost, he prefers not to stop for directions but to consult the map, keep driving, and find his way from the landmarks.

Doers generally have a "feel" for where they're going and how to find it. That sixth sense called a good sense of direction comes in handy in a new locale. They may use a map, but if they're merely told how to get there, they can find it. They figure if they get out and drive enough, they ought to be able to find the place.

how do you manage your house?

Another good indicator of your learning style is how you relate to your kids and spouse concerning housework, household routines, and order versus clutter. Although the following are examples of moms, the same characteristics apply to dads.

The visual parent's watchword is "a place for everything and everything in its place." Kathy, a visually oriented mom I know (a Watcher), values organization and order above all else. She's a perfectionist about how things look, especially her house. It's well-decorated, color-coordinated, and clutter-free. Notes, lists, and family papers are confined to the bulletin board or files in desk drawers, never piled on it. When you walk in, the home looks ready for a party.

Kathy decorated her child's room neatly with perfectly matched wallpaper and fabrics; she organized toys, games, and everything else on shelves and in special containers. She wants beds made before school every day and is easily annoyed by her child's lack of neatness in his room, which could escalate into a full-scale power struggle by the teenage years.

The house of the Talker/listener parent, Andrea, may seem a little cluttered, but she knows where things are and can concentrate on the task at hand even with a few stacked papers or piles on her desk. She can find what she needs and likes to see projects through. Communication and relationships are a top priority to Andrea, and her hospitality and openness make her home a favorite place for kids to gather after school.

An oft-repeated phrase from her to the kids is, "Let's talk about it." Often her son thinks she explains and talks too much. When problems arise, they are discussed in family meetings. She provides her children with CD players and their own CDs to listen to music and stories, and she is a natural storyteller. Besides reading books to her children, sharing many of her own fantasy tales and childhood recollections is a favorite pastime.

The Doer (mover) parent has a sign on her refrigerator: "I'd rather have a creative mess than tidy idleness." Of the three moms, she is the least concerned with order and the least bothered by clutter, but she is also probably the most fun. Vicki is a mom actively involved with her children, using her kitchen for projects like bread making and potting new plants.

Activity is the theme of her household—rollerblades (hers and the kids'), baseballs, gloves, and bicycles are out in the driveway and yard. A basket of knitting yarn and supplies are by the couch where she's been teaching her girls to knit, and rhythm instruments lie in another corner for impromptu music times. Vicki loves to take her children to the park and gets physically involved with them by running, swinging, and dancing around the living room when a favorite, lively song plays on the stereo. In fact, she participates on an adult soccer team on Saturdays and works out at the YMCA whenever she can.

An orderly, clean house takes a backseat to activity and time together with the children. All this fun is wonderful if her husband isn't a visual perfectionist whose main priority is order and who doesn't mind stepping over the latest project or exercise equipment sitting out on the living room floor.

a combination of styles

Perhaps you can't relate to only one style, but fit somewhere in between and possess a combination of strengths, like my friend Diane, who is a visual/kinesthetic (Watcher/Doer) parent. Her fortunate kids—the best of two styles is reflected in her parenting and household.

Although Diane loves beautiful colors and interesting furniture and collectibles in her home, the mood is flexible rather than structured, and people are more important to her than perfection. "We're always working on projects," says Diane. "Like last Friday, Charlie was out of school for teachers' conferences. We worked on collages with a variety of textures and paints on the dining room table."

Diane's hobby and part-time business is making original clay creations; she has a kiln in the garage to fire them. She also collects interesting things. Her boys like to make things, too, not structured crafts but creations out of paint and clay their mom provides. Her kinesthetic strengths show in how she's not afraid to try different things. Always experimenting, she doesn't follow plans for a craft or clay creation but works and plays with it until it "feels" right. Diane is outdoorsy and adventurous—her family camps, hikes, fishes, and bikes together. And her real love is working in the colorful cutting garden that takes up three-fourths of their front yard.

What about you? Do you do a lot of talking with your kids or expect them to read your mind? Is following visual directions difficult for you? Can you read any manual and figure out what to do? Are you an active parent like Vicki who can think of nothing more fun than playing a game of kickball with her kids?

Check the characteristics in the box below to discover your learning strengths:

kinesthetic "doer" parents

☐ Are quick to give hugs, pats on the back, and physical affection

☐ Tend to be involved in sports, working out, or keeping fit

☐ Show their emotions by their body language or actions

☐ Discipline their child by picking the child up or other physical action

☐ Don't like to sit for long meetings or lectures

auditory "talker" parents

☐ Discipline by telling the child what she has done wrong and explaining what she needs to do next time

☐ Do a lot of encouraging, praising, and explaining to the child

☐ Like listening to the radio, music, or CDs

☐ Show emotions by voice tone (sometimes unpleasantly shrill if really upset) and by words

☐ Like to sit close to the middle in a seminar so they can comment to their neighbors about what is said without disturbing the speaker

visual "watcher" parents

☐ Are quiet and don't say much when they are upset, but the children can tell by their facial expressions that they are really ticked off or perhaps sad

☐ Enjoy reading, movies, and television

☐ Discipline by giving "that look" or insisting the child have "time-out" in her room

☐ Like to sit close in a movie or up front in a seminar so they can see the speaker

Armed with this understanding about your learning style, you'll better perceive your child's learning differences. You'll also be able to eliminate many homework hassles and conflicts and unlock the potential of each child in your family, regardless of how she learns.

talkers and listeners

When Brittany was barely two years old, she would repeat word for word what her mother said. One day her mom, in her first few months of pregnancy, was lying on the couch, tired after errands with her daughter. Brittany wanted her to play, and Liz said, "I can't, honey. I'm totally exhausted, and you know when I get exhausted, I just have to rest."

When Brittany's dad got home, he said, "Let's go to the park."

Brittany replied, "I can't, Daddy. I'm totally exhausted, and you know when I get exhausted, I just have to rest!" This repetition was an everyday occurrence. Needless to say, they had to be very careful about what they said within Brittany's earshot.

Brittany also was fascinated with the sound and meaning of words. She asked about all kinds of words she heard spoken, read, or on television or radio. She also remembers songs heard in a movie only once and can sing them with the correct words and rhythm days or weeks later. Brittany has a sharp and sensitive recorder inside her mind taking note of everything she hears.

At five years old, she was the family's chatterbox, talking from the time her eyes open until she falls asleep. As much as her mother delights in her verbal ability, she sometimes looks forward to quiet evenings when the kids are in bed. But even at bedtime, Brittany chats with her baby sister in her crib and stuffed teddy bears and rabbits on the bed. She loves her series of Disney books with audiotapes and plays them over and over. Brittany enjoys drawing and art activities, but if given a choice will select musical activities, listening and singing along with tapes or the radio.

As a four-year-old, Brittany surprised her family by memorizing a whole chapter of the Bible to say at a church talent night, and the same night sang a duet with her dad. She has memorized poems and absorbs words like a sponge. When her mom read to her even as a toddler, if she missed a word, Brittany said, "No, that's not how it goes," and then would say what was on the page. After being read the story only a few times, she'd memorized it word for word.

This strong auditory learner with language talent will enjoy many aspects of school. In kindergarten Brittany is the first one to answer questions in class. Mentally processing the teacher's questions and verbalizing the answer is fun for her, and she can do it faster than anyone else in the class. She enjoys listening—to a point. But if she has to sit still and the teacher talks the whole class period, she finds the lack of interaction boring and likes to join in the talking. Children of this age still need movement and activity, and she is no exception. But Brittany will need to learn some patience and self-control—waiting for her turn to talk—and become an even better listener as she grows and begins formal schooling in a classroom situation.

Many academic situations are auditory, so in many classrooms this type of learner does well. When the teacher instructs and gives the class verbal directions, has class discussions on a regular basis, and asks questions to clarify the content, the student with verbal strengths has an advantage. He will also likely:

- Follow oral instructions after listening only once and won't need to hear things over and over

- Do well in tasks requiring phonetic analysis

- Learn to read most effectively with a phonics approach

- Love the read-aloud time of the school day

- Perform well verbally; do well with relating ideas and storytelling

- Enjoy music class, drama, and role-playing opportunities

- Appear brighter than test scores show him to be[1]

Talker/Listeners may be very language-talented but have handwriting problems or become frustrated by weaknesses such as difficulty with silent reading or poor spelling. In addition, they have a need for clear verbal explanations when given new or difficult material to learn, even if it's in a textbook, on a work sheet, or on the board. They can also become distracted by noise in the classroom or in the hall, and their love for talking to classmates can become a problem.

Brittany is like many children I've seen who are bright but

may not do well in school unless their parents and teachers understand and capitalize on their strengths, thus allowing them to perceive and understand the information, retain it, and be able to apply it.

You see, you can't memorize what you don't understand. If, for instance, your child can't comprehend math concepts by merely looking at numbers on a work sheet, you could demonstrate with beans and then discuss it and have your child put the ideas into his own words. If a chapter of history or science is difficult to comprehend through silent reading, ask your child to read it aloud or into a tape recorder.

What's important is to help your child understand the concepts and information by introducing them through her strength, and then transferring the information from short-term memory to long-term memory with some creative study strategies. Short-term memory holds information, words, or numbers just as long as they are visually before the class or as long as the student actively thinks about them. But once information moves into a child's long-term memory, it can be brought out, recalled, and applied to a test, or a real-life activity.

How does the information go from short-term memory to long-term memory? It takes repetition, but it doesn't have to be boring and tedious. The best learning takes place when we use the child's strengths rather than weaknesses in the practice and drill. Just reading multiplication tables (2 x 1 = 2, 2 x 2 = 4) silently may be boring to a child who is verbally oriented and needs to hear and say—or maybe even sing—the times tables.

One of the best approaches for maximum learning is to start with your child's strongest style of learning, reinforce it with his secondary strength, and finally, use the new information in a creative way. For the creative part, for example, ask students to make up a poem with states and capitals, or to make up a game. Any creative method works and will boost achievement enormously.[2]

Let's look at some strategies for learning with listening, talking, rehearsing, tape-recording, and other strategies.

studying in style

One night our daughter Alison had thirty irregular verb forms to memorize—present, past, and past perfect tenses—ninety words in all. She had missed the explanation, drill, and practice in class due to illness, so at first the task looked overwhelming. I went over the list orally with her, having her say the words. Then I showed her how to make a tape recording of each verb and its forms. Alison enjoyed making the tape and then played it over several times, reciting along with the tape until the sounds were firmly fixed in her mind. She was seeing the words, hearing them, and saying them, which made a stronger imprint on her memory. I gave her a practice test I had written out before bedtime, circling the verbs she missed, and she studied those words, saying them aloud. The whole study session took approximately forty-five minutes.

The next morning, Alison got her tape recorder out while she was dressing and practiced the verb forms again. That day, she made an A on the test and came home with greatly boosted confidence and motivation. She needed to practice hearing and saying the information to do her best and began to use tape-recording to study for geography, French, and other subjects.

"When does a learning style become a learning deficit or disability?" I asked my friend Steve, a psychologist.

"For me," he said, "it happens when you don't let me use my auditory strengths! That's the way I've always learned best."

So, too, with children who have auditory and verbal strengths. Let's capitalize on these strengths, help them take a different approach when they have to master new or difficult information, and watch them achieve. Here's how:

make your own study tape

Just as Alison found, a blank tape and tape recorder is a wonderful study tool for children with auditory strengths. Kinesthetic learners enjoy using it too, especially if they can listen to the tape with a Walkman and move around during their oral practice.

First, have the child make flash cards out of index cards (with questions on one side and answers on the other) or use flash cards from a learning store. To make the tape, the student asks a question into the microphone, waits five or more seconds, and then goes on to the next question. After the tape is made, the child plays it back and inserts the answer after each question. This boosts understanding and memory, as the child sees the fact, says it, and hears it. The study-tape method can be used in any subject, from simple addition facts and multiplication tables to French vocabulary and states and capitals.

Tape-recording chapters of textbooks, class notes, and lectures also helps the verbal learner master the material. It can also aid reading comprehension. When Joseph read silently, he didn't comprehend his history or literature. His mom had him read his work into a tape recorder and then play it back to himself. By doing this, his grades came up a letter in each subject.

Even for older students, tape-recording is useful. Although Ann is a good student in her first year of law school, she finds that when she tape-records her twenty-page outline of notes on each course before the final and then plays it back several times, she makes higher grades and has better overall mastery.

Sherry, a homeschooling mother, makes a daily tape of instructions for the day's lessons for her daughter Laura. She can slow the tape down or listen to it again if she needs to. For example, Sherry reads the phonics rule, gives Laura several examples, tells her which page to turn to in the workbook, and includes specific encouragement—"I know you know this part; let's go over it one more time." Then she goes on to the math instructions and other subjects for the day. This has enabled Laura to be more independent and yet have clear directions in her home study.

Tape recording shouldn't totally replace oral instruction. A short time spent asking the child questions and having the child answer them out loud can be multiplied back in the retention and understanding gained. It also helps you keep in touch with what your child is learning and provides a springboard for discussion of the topic.

making poems and songs out of information

Setting information to music helps with recall and retrieval. Music is a powerful learning tool. Researchers and therapists have found that even when people have lost the ability to speak, they can learn all over again when phrases are set to music.[3] Most of us learned our ABCs with the ABC song. You may have learned the books of the Bible or the state capitals with a song.

The rhythm and rhyme of poetry works in a similar way to aid memory, especially for language-oriented learners. In phrases such as "In fourteen hundred and ninety-two Columbus sailed the ocean blue" and "Thirty days has September, April, June, and November," we learned information and can recall it years later. "I before E except after C or when sounded as A as in neighbor and weigh," came in handy to spell many words correctly.

When I was in ninth grade, we were to create a poster that illustrated an algebraic concept. I drew a garden with bright flowers (each had an algebra formula inside) and a sun-bonneted girl watering them with her tilted-over watering can. The verse I made up went like this:

> "Mary, Mary, quite contrary
> How do your polynomials subtract?
> You change the sign of the subtrahend,
> Then add as a matter of fact."

Although I've forgotten a lot of other algebra over the years through lack of use, I haven't forgotten that formula or the verse, so embedded is it in my memory. Help your kids develop songs or poems to remember information. If they come up with the words and/or melody, and add a picture, they'll remember it better. Tape-recording the song or poem to review later is great reinforcement.

learn with both sides of the brain

To say someone is totally right-brained or left-brained is an over-simplification. We all use both sides of the brain in learning and working on a day-to-day basis. But just as we have a tendency to use one hand or foot more than the other, most people's thinking favors one hemisphere of the brain. The left side functions mainly in analyzing incoming data in a logical, sequential way, and de-coding and interpreting language. The right side functions in cre-ative processes, mental images, emotions, and music, to name a few. The right hemisphere is involved with thinking for visual and spatial tasks. The left processes in a step-by-step way, while the right tends to process all at once, looking for patterns and con-necting things into a whole.

"By using the whole brain approach," said Dr. Wanda Draper, psychiatrist and professor at the University of Oklahoma Medical School, "you are using the right hemisphere to map out or illus-trate what the left hemisphere has reasoned or deduced."[4] She and other experts maintain that when you use these two parts of the brain together you increase your thinking capacity, under-standing, and retention. Combine music and language and you'll be helping kids learn with both sides of the brain.

Another example of two-sided learning would be to draw diagrams, maps, and charts to represent concepts or stick figures to represent historical characters as a part of note-taking in a class lecture or a home-study session. Encourage your child to picture what she's studying while asking herself: What are the key words and ideas? Why are they important to the main topic?[5]

enhancing visual abilities

Verbal/auditory people often don't rely on visual abilities. They may not even be aware of seeing pictures in their mind's eye, and may need practice generating pictures. They need to be challenged, however, to develop visual capacities because these thinking skills provide great help (and save time) in remembering many different kinds of information in certain areas—such as math facts and formulas, spelling words, geography, geometry, and history.

Just as listening skills are needed to excel in the classroom and in real-life job situations, making pictures is a helpful tool for much academic learning as well. After drawing a time line or a chart of the planets and their characteristics, the child could verbalize it and discuss the concepts and connections.

A good method for learning lines of poetry or speeches is to write the sentence on the board. Have the student say the verse or sentence aloud. Erase one word and have him say the sentence and try to picture the words in his mind's movie screen. Repeat, erasing another word. Continue in the same way until all the words are gone. Have the child say it in its entirety and check with the original sentence.

Combining modalities in these ways—especially verbal and visual—enhances learning. Several studies at the UCLA Graduate School of Education showed that students recall information and words better when a verbal and visual activity is used. Research showed that students remembered vocabulary words better when they read the definitions and drew their own pictures to represent them than when they merely read the words and wrote the definitions. Part of the study also involved teaching kinetic molecular theory (which is extremely complex) to kindergarten and elementary children using pictures, concrete examples, and verbal explanation. All concepts were represented visually. With concrete examples, the children could relate to and connect with something they were familiar with. The results were impressive—almost 70 percent of the children learned and remembered the concepts a year after the experiment.[6]

In the chapter on visual learning you'll find more visual methods such as mapping and diagramming techniques.

mnemonics

Mnemonics or "memory aids" are techniques to improve the memory. Just like any other part of the body, the memory gets better the more we exercise it. One good way to exercise the memory is to make an acrostic. An acrostic allows you to remember a list of words by taking the first letter from each word and substituting another word beginning with that same letter. For example, to memorize the seven continents:

Africa	Aunt
Asia	Alice
Australia	Ate
Antarctica	Apples
North America	Nearly
Europe	Every
South America	Sunday

The sentence "Aunt Alice ate apples nearly every Sunday" serves as a reminder for the names of the continents.

Acronyms are another mnemonic aid. To memorize a list of words using an acronym, take the first letter of each word and make a new word from each of those letters. For example, you can remember the elements of a short story by the acronym SCAT (setting, characters, action, theme) or the order of scientific classification by "King Phillip came over for green spaghetti" (kingdom, phylum, class, order, family, genus, species).

As one educator said, "There are no poor memories, only poor learning habits!" Memory is vastly improved by using strategies to organize the information—thus moving the information from short-term to long-term memory (the brain's file cabinet). If your child or a study group makes up their own acrostic, it's even more effective, and the sillier and more humorous, exaggerated, or colorful, the better. A chain of silly words that forms a sentence works the same way. Some students made up the following:

- "Never eat sour wieners" for the directions north, east, south, west.

- "Dad made sweet bread" for the steps in division: divide, multiply, subtract, and bring down.

Mnemonics can be made up in any subject: language arts, math, science, social studies. These can help your child remember the colors of the spectrum, the names of the planets, or the order of the metric system: "King Henry doesn't milk dairy cows Monday" (K-kilo, H-hecta, D-deca, M-meter, D-deci, C-centi, M-milli).

concentration

This game improves visual memory, which often needs strengthening in auditory learners. It also provides a good chance for interaction and going over the questions orally. To play, all the questions and answers are written on one side of colored blank cards—the question on one card, the answer on another—and then randomly placed facedown on the floor or table. The first player turns over two cards, trying to match a question with the correct answer. If the player gets a match, she gets to keep the cards and is rewarded with another turn. If the player turns over mismatched cards, she returns the cards, facedown, to the same position on the floor or table, and the next player takes a turn. The play continues until all the cards have been matched together. The player with the most cards at the end wins.

jumpstarting writing assignments

If your child has difficulty getting started or has writer's block on an assignment, Talkers do best by brainstorming verbally about the topic and writing the ideas in cluster form with the idea in the middle and connecting thoughts written around it like spokes on a wheel. Rehearsing, or talking through the ideas, is one of the best prewriting strategies for kids with auditory strengths.

If the assignment is a personal-experience story, your child could tell it first into a tape recorder, then play the tape back and fill in missing details or rearrange events in chronological order, writing them down. After the written narrative has gotten "cold"—that is, put away for a few hours or a day—have her read aloud the story, revise, add missing details, and edit. A quick-find word guide (or spell-check on a computer) can be used to check and correct the spelling of words.

math strategies

Kids can make cassette tapes of story problems in addition to the written-down problem or accompanying picture. In addition, writing in math can be helpful to verbal students. They can make up their own story problem that involves addition, multiplication, and subtraction. Or they can write an addition problem that equals a given answer, like 555, for example. Rewriting an assigned story problem in their own words clarifies the thought processes and helps students come up with a problem-solving strategy.

Clustering can be used in math to represent and organize information to be learned. To review and prepare for a test on fractions, for example, the student and his study group could brainstorm and discuss everything they know about fractions. One student writes "FRACTIONS" in the middle of a big sheet of paper. Around it the student then writes information such as "Ways to write fractions," followed by a list of these ways; "Ways fractions are used and applied in real world," followed by a list; and "Functions you can do with fractions" (addition, subtraction, division, multiplication, reducing, and so on).[7] Writing in math is a great way to boost comprehension of concepts and retention.

Students can also describe things in words, like a geometric shape: "A rectangle has four sides and its corners are all right angles." Then they try to "see" what they have described in words. Students need not only to see the problem worked on the board but also to hear the teacher talk through the problem-solving process.

reading material aloud

Reading material aloud, whatever the age of the auditory/verbal student, is always helpful. It aids in clarifying ideas and enables the student to get a "big picture" and a better understanding of the concepts. Alternate with your child reading a chapter that's been assigned—parent reads a paragraph or page, then student reads a paragraph or page. Even if just the first few pages of a chapter are read aloud and discussed briefly in this way, it will increase comprehension of the material.

a little help from my friends

A home study group before a big test or exam is invaluable, especially for junior high and high school Talker/Listeners. The best study groups have a few hardworking classmates who want to do well on the test. In saying the information aloud in their study group, they'll understand it better. They'll inspire each other's efforts and stir up a little competition. They can orally go over the material; discuss ideas, key words, and concepts; and quiz each other.

boosting talker/listener skills in preschoolers

The foundations we build before children start first grade are vitally important. Readiness for reading, language building, and foundations for math skills all take place in the preschool years. Here are some ways to enhance auditory learning in young children:

what doesn't belong?

Name four objects like a kitty, bird, hat, and dog. Have your child listen, and then ask, "Which thing doesn't belong here?" Then list a different group of things—a jacket, table, glove, and sock—and repeat the question, "What doesn't belong?"

i spy

Each player, in turn, looks around the room (or car or outside) and says, "I spy something green." The other players attempt to identify the "something." The one who guesses correctly gets to be the spy on the next turn.

write your own story

Set out photographs of your child and your family. Ask your child to make up a story about each picture, while you write down what she is dictating. When your child is finished, read the story aloud, tape-record it, and then bind it together with yarn or staples into a book.

fill in the story

Read your child a story, occasionally saying "blank" instead of a word in the story. Ask your child to fill in the "blank" with a word that he thinks will work in the context of the sentence.

In the next chapter we'll look at energetic Doers—their strengths, and your strategies to help them learn and achieve.

doers and touchers

One day when he was five, Aaron spent the afternoon at his grandmother's house. While she was out of the room, he was supposed to be playing with his cars. But when she returned, she realized her prize figurine's arms and legs were broken off.

"Why did you do this?" Aaron's grandmother asked. "You've broken my antique figurine!"

"I just wanted to see if the arms moved. I wanted to see if the legs moved or if it would bend," Aaron said. Inquisitive Aaron had no intention of causing a problem or ruining anything. He was just a "Doer"—a "toucher" through and through.

The way Aaron and similar kids learn often gets them into trouble. Think of the story of inventor Thomas Edison, who while trying to imitate birds, once sat on a nest of eggs and smashed them all. Aaron's hands-on way of finding out how things work also meant dismantling the remote-control car he got at Christmas and taking apart Mom's toaster when it wouldn't pop the toast up. However, he did put it back together and even fixed it! Although he's now the best swimmer on the YMCA swim team and a gymnast who has already won several youth competitions, Aaron is restless when he has to sit for long periods at his desk doing pencil-and-paper seat work, and has been assigned to the low reading group for second grade.

Cary is another student who was having trouble with some basic scientific concepts. After Cary's teacher taught cell division, assigned a chapter to read in the textbook, and handed out a work sheet to finish, Cary read through everything and still didn't understand. Her grade on the quiz was only a sixty, not enough to pass. That week her tutor pulled out some clay and made a model of a cell while explaining and demonstrating the difference between animal and plant cell division. Then she let Cary show and explain the concepts of cell division using the clay. She let her use a pen to mark the chromosomes. When her mom picked her up at the end of the tutoring session, Cary showed her the cell and told her what she had learned. Usually she had trouble explaining things, but with the three-dimensional clay cell, she communicated it clearly and glowed with pride. Her grade on the test rose to a B.

Lauree, another Doer, was not interested in the chapter on the human body until she got to dissect a chicken. When her mom turned the material into a hands-on approach and she got to feel the muscles, identify the bones by touch, and then write them down, the subject came alive to her.

Her older brother John said, "Oh, gross!" while she cut into the chicken. He'd rather just read about it and write a report. But Lauree's active curiosity was engaged by the dissection. She also loves to put together "potions" from the kitchen and see what happens in the chemical reactions. When reading, she gets distracted easily. When they read aloud as a family, they've found that she concentrates and enjoys the story or chapter much more when she can do something with her hands, such as draw a picture of what they are reading about.

Children with kinesthetic and tactile strengths are active, hands-on learners. They process knowledge through physical sensations. "Kinesthetic" strength means the child learns things best by doing them; the whole body is involved in the learning activity. "Tactile" strength means learning is enhanced by touching and manipulating equipment or material. Sometimes students are both tactile and kinesthetic, but not always. Since the study methods that follow in this chapter generally work just as well for both kinds of active learners, I will refer to them interchangeably.

Lauree, Cary, and Aaron, all Doers, are the most at risk for frustration at school and home because the majority of instruction, and many of the tasks and testing, are auditory and visual—it's not because they aren't bright. Their strengths are in the kinesthetic area. Their high energy levels often try our patience. They aren't able to sit still long. Their difficulty with abstract concepts challenges our teaching methods. But they have tremendous potential and intelligence, if we just learn how to teach them, show them how to capitalize on their strengths, and compensate for their weaknesses.

Sometimes just a modification of a study strategy will make the difference. Adapting assignments can motivate kids to do their best. All kids work well with hands-on activities and manipulatives, but especially our Doers. Steven caught on to the math functions and mastered his math facts rapidly when his mom supplemented his math instruction with Touch Math (see TouchMath.com for information). Cary's tutor has her write her acrostics in salt to increase her retention. "If I just have her say aloud the acrostic 'Can Cherry speak?' for three types of clouds—cirrus, cumulus, and stratus—she forgets it, but when she writes it in salt, she can get it right on the test and remember it the next week." Capitalizing on her kinesthetic strengths has boosted not only her grades but also her self-esteem.

A kinesthetic learner may be strong in the following:

- Fine and gross motor balance (or may be better at gross, or large muscle, coordination and balance)

- Rhythmic movement

- Identifying and matching objects

- Taking gadgets apart and putting them back together again

- Using concrete objects as learning aids

- Three-dimensional thinking

- Creativity, problem solving, and seeing the connection between ideas

The computer in many of these kids' brains keeps their movements timed perfectly in a gymnastic performance or crucial soccer kick. They have excellent motor memory. They enjoy doing things with their hands, touch everything in their path, and get up and walk around frequently in a classroom. Thus, they may be the first picked for the baseball team, but they're not the teacher's pet. They often communicate more with body language and gestures than words. They are the best at cutting out cardboard letters for the class bulletin board, and assemble puzzles and other materials well. But they may have difficulty counting by rote or sequencing materials without concrete objects to count, and learning abstract symbols such as letters or math symbols is difficult without manipulatives or real-life experiences.

Albert Einstein once said, "Knowledge is experience— everything else is just information." How can we encourage and facilitate the learning of our bright, hands on kids?

hands-on learning

"Rather than fight their natural learning style, why not use it to help kids uncover the patterns in the universe?" asks Elaine Gaines, learning specialist. "The real world, tangible things, hands-on stuff are the 'textbooks and work sheets' of mathematics for children," she adds. Elaine observes that kids are inundated with math work sheets, workbooks, and textbooks and are made to memorize masses of information that mean nothing to them because from ages five to twelve children learn and think concretely rather than abstractly.[1]

This problem applies to all children, but especially to those who have kinesthetic strengths and a three-dimensional thinking style. With just pencil-and-paper activities, their learning and motivation plummets. Research from learning centers and neurologists shows that many people with great intelligence in the three-dimensional realm—the world-renowned inventor, actor, engineer, or Olympic gold-medal winner—have trouble with two-dimensional academic tasks (like deciphering printed words, numbers, and symbols in textbooks and on work sheets).[2] Doers learn best when they touch, see, hear, and experience real-life things. For example, the concept of one-third will be best understood and internalized after they divide one candy bar into three parts; the symbol 20¢, by counting two out of ten dimes for the savings bank; or by counting three leaves on five clovers to demonstrate 3 x 5 = 15 leaves.[3]

If we can use hands-on learning methods at the highest levels of education, such as medical school and graduate-school research, why can't we use them during the crucial elementary years when it matters the most?[4] The more we can return to hands-on instruction, the more children will achieve. Provide buttons, packages of sticks, muffin cups, and beans for counting and performing math functions. Have firsthand experiments when studying electricity, insects, or other science areas. Dissect flowers and then label the parts. Get a frog hatchery kit or an ant farm.

Go from the concrete to the concept and then to the abstract (figuring the problem out on paper). Let's apply this principle of hands-on learning to other tasks kids must tackle. For when we do—as the mom did who made the stuffed alphabet letters her daughter Karen could feel, play, and spell with—we find they can excel and grow in confidence of their learning ability.

"Parenting a kinesthetic child is hard work," said Gretchen. "But the rewards are fantastic." Karen became a fine student, cooperative and happy, but her mom admits there is an investment of time. She couldn't memorize the multiplication tables by just sitting down and reading silently over them or saying them to herself. "It takes more time to be involved than to say, 'Learn your multiplication tables yourself,'" said her mom.

She mastered addition and subtraction by counting rocks and little blocks, and the rougher the texture of an object, the more it held her attention. Karen learned the multiplication tables better by walking around the house reciting and being quizzed with flash cards while riding in the car. She has a marvelous attention span when she can be actively involved with things.

learning to think visually

Even kinesthetic students who don't naturally perceive things visually can improve their visual memory and thinking skills. Actor Tom Cruise faced dyslexia and accompanying reading problems in his growing-up years in school. Always in remedial classes— in fifteen different schools, because of moving—his problems worsened. His mother, who had special-education training, recognized his need and helped him overcome his learning problems. The strategy was learning to focus his attention and learning to think visually. "I became very visual," Cruise said, "and learned to create mental images in order to comprehend what I read."[5] He also learned he had to work harder than everyone else to make it. By extra effort and improving his visual skills, he brought his reading up to grade level by his junior year of high school.

Visual cues will help the kinesthetic learner. Post a picture of what your child's room looks like when it is clean on your child's bulletin board or door and it will give her a pattern when it's time to sort through the rubble. Tape a picture of a place setting with fork, spoon, knife, and plate inside a cupboard door to aid setting the table properly.

reading

The most important task of every child is to learn to read effectively, to build reading comprehension and speed. Yet learning to read can be a challenge for many Doers. Chapter 8 has suggestions on reading methods that work for kids who learn best by movement or touch. Let me encourage you to do all you can to not let your child fall into being the poorest reader or accept a "reading disabled" label. Instead, find a method that builds on your child's strengths and meets his needs. Capitalize on his interests or what he wants to learn about—and he can become a good reader.

learning boards

A white, dry-erase board in your child's room is a great resource. Sliding closet doors can even be painted with chalkboard paint. The learning board can be used to work math problems, outline a chapter in any subject, brainstorm for ideas, or draw a large mind map. On it your child can practice larger movements in writing spelling words or answers being studied for a test. Writing in small lines is often frustrating for movers but on a big board is fun. Let your child write the words in the air and then on the board as she says each letter in the word, and then the whole word. She can trace the letters with two fingers until the word is erased. The night before the test, a parent can call out each word while the child writes it on the board for a practice test.

And best of all, the board can be used to "teach" the material to the family the night before a test. With this active way of studying, kids can internalize the concepts as they explain them to someone else. Research shows that learners who teach information to other people retain 90 percent of it.[6] The child may even discover she enjoys teaching. Kinesthetic learners can make the most dynamic, effective teachers.

math for active kids

Kids with kinesthetic strengths who are pushed too early into abstract math concepts and symbols, made to memorize by rote, and apply concepts they don't understand often develop "math phobia." Although they may have potential to be excellent math students, they are being taught backward. Math should be taught—especially to these kids—from the concrete to the abstract. Let them pour a half gallon of water into quart jars and pint measuring bottles to see how much the jars and bottles equal. Have her measure the walls of her bedroom with measuring tape to see how many inches equals a yard and how many feet are in the perimeter of her room. The more your mover can experience hands-on math, the more concepts she can understand and master.

And the more you can build solid foundations incorporating math into everyday life before your child starts school, the better. Here are some excellent ways:

- Learning a pattern. Family chores and activities such as sorting laundry, sorting silverware, and setting the table are good practice in learning a pattern (a fundamental math skill) and categorizing. Children can count toys while putting them away in bins or shelves, count out cookies and apples, or count SUVs while traveling.

- Learning what's alike and what's different. One of the most important concepts preschoolers need to learn is what's alike and what's different, what's greater than and what's less than, and the best way to learn it is with concrete objects and everyday things. Put several objects out in a row and ask, "Which one is different?" Fill three glasses with different amounts of water and ask, "Which one has more?" As you see things in the neighborhood and on errands, ask, "How are the things alike? How are they different? Which is biggest?"

- Reasoning skills. When you're reading to your child, pause before the end and ask, "What will happen next?" This gives your child an opportunity to develop deductive reasoning skills and a sense of direction in math thinking and problem solving.

- Finding the missing part. Another vital skill is to find the missing part. Ask, "All of our family is not here; how many are gone?" "There were six sodas in the refrigerator; now there are only two. How many are missing?" This lays the groundwork for algebra concepts like finding the missing variable.

manipulatives at home

When Kathy's son Dave couldn't understand how addition and subtraction connect, she got some plastic centimeter rods of different colors, wrote the numbers on the corresponding rods, and then had him add and subtract some numbers. After only a few minutes, the lightbulb went on. While manipulating the rods, he instantly understood the concept, whereas when he looked at symbols and numbers on a page in his math workbook, he couldn't get it. You can find math manipulatives at learning stores or education sites on the Internet.

When seven-year-old Jannea has items to count—Lego blocks, bingo markers, buttons—she does much better in math. Little red balls that fit on pegs for a bingo game helped her see and feel when she was counting by fives. One mom used peanut butter sandwiches to teach the distributive properties of multiplication.

$$3(A + B) = 3A + 3B$$
Peanut Butter (White Bread + Dark Bread)
$$P(W + D) = PW + PD$$

Manipulatives are not childish and can be used with any age student. High school science and math teachers of physics, chemistry, calculus, and geometry have found that their students, no matter how bright, find manipulatives challenging to make and motivating to use.

For early computation skills, you can also buy or make a big stack of number cards, including five zeros, five ones, five twos, and so forth up to ten. Then you can make up games that offer practice in calculating. You pick a card (four) and your child picks a card (six) and you each count out the right number of buttons (or bingo counters or other colored objects) for your card. Then see who has more and who has less.

Hang up a string across the room and let your child clothespin numbers up in order. Clip two numbers up—twenty-five at one end and forty at the other. Then call out a number and have your child clip it up where it goes. Continue in this fashion until all the numbers are in order. Ordering numbers and putting a value to them is an important skill.

Once your ideas get going, the sky's the limit on all the ways you can help your child get hands-on practice in math. At the grocery store, your child can practice estimating your bill, redeeming coupons, and weighing produce on the big scales. You can call attention to batting averages in the newspaper for your athletically minded child. Lemonade stands and money-making businesses are great ways for kids to learn about money and profits.

get creative

Here are some more strategies to help movers learn skills they need to succeed in school:

- Spelling snakes—Print spelling words on a laminated piece of construction paper. Roll out "snakes" or long pieces of clay. The student puts clay over the letters so that the spelling words are written with clay.

- Cookie-sheet words—Write spelling words with play dough or shaving cream, or in cornmeal on a cookie sheet.

- Globe find—Your child and a friend each have a globe. Call out a country, ocean, or continent, and say, "Go." The one who runs across the room and places her finger on the correct spot on the globe first wins that round. You can also drill your child individually.

- Map find—With a U.S. map, call out a capital, abbreviation, motto, or state nickname and say, "Go." Your child runs over to the map and touches the correct state to gain a point.

- A portable magnetic drawing/writing board—This is a great to write spelling words or practice working math problems. You can find them in toy and learning stores (good in car, desk, or small space).

- Rap song or cheer—Make up a rap or cheer with spelling or vocabulary words. Putting words together with big movements, rhyme, and language is a dynamic combination.

- Puzzles—Puzzles are great for learning the fifty states and the continents.

- Sign language—One child I know had a hard time with spelling. Her mom taught her sign language in the fourth grade, and from then on when she studied, she spelled them aloud while simultaneously spelling them in sign language. She immediately learned and remembered the words.

- Simon Says—This game is good practice in following directions while integrating movement and play. The person being Simon says to the players, "Simon says pat your head while jumping up and down four times." Players do the actions only if the leader says, "Simon says" before the instruction.

games for learning

Making a game with material to be studied involves creativity and higher-order thinking skills. It also is a great way to reinforce vocabulary, organize information, and increase comprehension of the material—in any subject. The game can be as simple as a crossword puzzle, word bingo, or a board game with a spinner.

First the student gathers together the textbook, class notes, old quizzes, study cards, and any handouts on the material to be studied. Cardboard, poster board, or even a manila file folder can be used for the playing board. The board can be laminated. The path of spaces can be made with ruler and felt-tip markers. Dice, spinner, and pieces to move around the board, if it is a board game, are essential; glue, tape, ruler, and other materials will also be helpful in making the game. The child does the artwork (it could be a cooperative or group venture). Then there needs to be someone with whom to play the game—a classmate, sibling, or parent.

Board games, checkers and chess, and playing cards are also excellent ways for Doers to learn math and language concepts and get practice with thinking skills they need to handle many intellectual tasks.

organizational skills for doers

Organizational skills are important for all students, but active learners, who usually tend to be scattered with their papers and books, need them most of all. At the secondary level the number-one reason for failure is disorganization, especially for Doers. Jackie Kelly, a special education teacher and private tutor, told me about the tenth-grade girl referred to her for evaluation and tutoring, because the school suspected she was "learning disabled." Upon testing her, Jackie found she had no diagnosable disability. But she was so scattered and disorganized—class notes all over the place, a textbook lost—she couldn't even pull together her materials to study for a test. No wonder she was failing. Once she got an organizational system that worked for her, her grades came up.

Here are some organizational tips:

- Especially for younger children, allow a break for playtime after school before homework is started. Movers need to get the wiggles out before being still for another period of time.

- Let your child decorate a homework station, a corner or desk away from the distraction of television, with bright bins, colored file folders, and a bulletin board to tack up assignments.

- Break study time into doable bites by helping divide homework into short sections. Time the sessions, and after twenty minutes (or task completed) have a break for a snack or to play with the dog, then finish homework.

- Supply your child with a homework backpack with dividers—one pouch for teacher notes and completed homework and one pouch for books and notebook—and designate a specific place by the door to put "school stuff" for the next day.

reading and riding

If you have a stationary bike, your child could ride it while reading a book propped up on a handlebar stand. Teachers who've let reluctant readers try biking and reading simultaneously find it increased their speed and comprehension. Movers also read better while rocking in a rocking chair. Or let your child do active studying by jumping on a rebounder or throwing plastic darts into a bulls-eye while you call out geography facts or history questions.

The student who needs movement can make audiotapes of the notes or questions to be studied and then listen to them on a Walkman. That way, he can hear and verbally practice the information while walking, running, or jumping.

Since kids can't always use an active approach for all classroom assignments, it's important to develop and use your child's secondary strength. If that is visual, try some visual study strategies. If it is auditory, develop and enhance that modality.

encouraging preschoolers or kids with low mover skills

Some children who may have strong visual or auditory skills may lack fine or large motor skills. Here are some ways to enhance and develop those physical abilities:

- Provide objects for developing physical coordination, such as playground equipment, a balance beam, balls, riding toys, beanbags, and a Ping-Pong table for an older child. In addition, all kids need chances to skip, hop, jump rope, and catch and throw a ball.

- Take your preschooler to toddler aerobic classes at a local community center or enroll in gym and physical development programs such as Gymboree, which is great for developing coordination and motor skills.

- Arts and crafts activities, making origami, cutting snowflakes, painting, or stringing beads help develop fine motor skills.

- Both preschoolers and kids who are active learners often struggle with staying on task. Increase your child's concentration and on-task focus by regularly working together on a mini-project from start to finish. For example, a game of pick-up sticks calls for patience, skill, and only fifteen minutes of quality time together. But that short time of focusing on doing one thing—putting together a puzzle, painting a picture, or making a simple craft—will help develop the ability to focus in the classroom, which is crucial to school success.

- Provide a lot of hugs, pats, and physical affection. All children need affection but Doer kids have a greater need for physical affirmation that doesn't diminish as they grow. Joy, a mother of two, found that her six-year-old daughter had a definite need for physical contact when tackling difficult work. Instead of shooing her off, Joy found when she just stands beside her daughter's chair at the table and puts her arm around her or sits beside her, her daughter is infused with courage to deal with new information she's tackling on her homeschool work. "This proximity seems to provide reassurance," she said. "I've put two and two together. My daughter may simply be trying to reestablish a degree of closeness that was abruptly interrupted during my difficult pregnancy and the first two years of our caring for our son with cerebral palsy. In any case, the physical touch is helping her now."

Sometimes just a touch or pat on the shoulder can help a child refocus on her tasks. As you adapt hands-on study methods like those in this chapter to your child's active learning style, you'll find your child will become more aware of how she learns and remembers best. In the next chapter, we will look at visual learning and ways to enhance visual skills in your child.

watchers

Holly noticed her mom's new dress before anyone else in the family. From an early age she told stories that were rich in pictorial imagery and description. When her parents asked how she thought up the story, she said, "It's just the movie going on in my mind!" Because of her visual skills, Holly was an excellent student in most subjects in elementary school, especially spelling. After looking at a list of twenty words a few times, she could spell them almost perfectly. "Spelling was so easy because I could read the words off a screen in my mind just like someone was holding it up. It's not like I had to work at thinking how the word sounded."

Chris, our middle son, was entertained by his surroundings, by seeing people, by his fascination with colors and shapes of things as a baby. He didn't need action going on all the time to be happy. He could beat me anytime on word finds and large multipiece puzzles. He was exceptionally observant, had a great imagination, and loved dressing up in costumes he made and pretending he was a firefighter, Corporal Rusty, or an Indian chief.

As an honor high school student with an excellent visual memory, Chris received only one criticism from his teachers: He was "too quiet" in class (some teachers would give anything for a class of quiet kids!). Several said he didn't ask enough questions or participate enough in discussions. An independent student, he said some of his favorite times of learning came from reading the *World Book Encyclopedia* from volumes A to Z. By age eight, he had read almost every volume, on a myriad of subjects he was curious about. He would rather learn about something by reading about it or analyzing it in his own mind rather than listening to someone talk on and on in a lecture. And from the many pictures he drew in childhood to the four years of art he took in high school, creating sculptures, watercolors, and designs remained one of his favorite pastimes.

"If I have a list of German vocabulary words to memorize for an exam," said Tiffany, a visually oriented college student, "I study the list, study my notes, and then if I think or hear the German words, I see the English equivalent as if written on a piece of paper." For oral exams, if she rereads the German stories and conversations, she is able to repeat almost the exact text because she remembers what it looked like on the page. Tiffany has a better visual memory for words than numbers or pictures. She is not art-oriented, and her second strongest modality is auditory—her favorite subjects being German, Spanish, public speaking, and English literature.

Students like Holly, Chris, and Tiffany have visual skills that they have learned to use in the classroom. Some visual students remember words best, some recall pictures best, some call up numbers best, and some all three—words, pictures, and numbers. When you try to read them something, this type of learner says, "Let me see it on the page." When you tell them how to do something, they say, "Show me and I'll do it!" They like to see what they are learning. They work best at uncluttered desks for full concentration. They also benefit from illustrations, diagrams, and charts and often make pictures to symbolize concepts when taking notes.

helping students harness visual strengths

Some students have good visual abilities but haven't learned to use them in academics. Judy was a creative artist, could recreate a still-life drawing from figures on the table in art class, and make pictures in her mind easily when reading her favorite ski or fitness magazines, but when it came to transferring these visual abilities to the mounds of reading she had to do for history, English, and life science, she drew a blank. Many students like Judy can harness these skills in visual learning to maximize their study time and achieve more at school.

Jared loves pictures, baseball cards, drawing, and fixing things. He can see a picture or diagram and put together whatever the directions show. In the car, he sees landmarks and details and asks, "Dad, did you see that sign?" However, Jared had a tendency to procrastinate in his schoolwork. He'd dawdle and doodle around with a ten-minute task for thirty or forty-five minutes. When his mom, Sherry, began to capitalize on visual abilities, he got a lot more done. She now writes all of his assignments down with a time limit and gives him a kitchen timer. "This spelling list will take you fifteen minutes. This math sheet will take you approximately thirty minutes."

To help him stay organized, Jared's mom uses a different color of paper for each subject's work—history, green; language arts, yellow—and color-codes it to a matching folder. He makes illustrated time lines in history and posters and models of concepts in science. She uses yellow sticky notes to remind him of chores he needs to do around the house. With the new ways of working, he's getting twice as much done.

visual learners in the classroom

Some of a visually strong student's skills are a great benefit in the classroom. A student with visual strengths remembers approximately 70 to 75 percent of what she sees or reads the first time. The visual student:

- has a good sight vocabulary; uses picture clues in reading

- keeps an organized desk and remembers where to put things back

- scores well on standardized, multiple-choice, and matching tests

- usually becomes a rapid reader and has good comprehension

- can follow directions on work sheets, diagrams, and written-down instructions

- often excels in map skills and math computation

- likes to work puzzles, word finds, and visual games

- prefers art class to music class[1]

However, in the classroom, visual learners often get frustrated with oral drill. Josh's third-grade math teacher started the "Twenty Second Club," in which students became official members if they could say the multiplication families in twenty seconds. The children practiced at home and said them in front of the class while the teacher checked off the family groups. When all students reached the twelve family, she planned to throw a pizza party. This was a wonderful activity for the auditory learners. They loved it and were the first to make the "Twenty Second Club." But Josh still hadn't made the club after his third week of trying.

Visual learners should realize that while they learn fast, they can forget equally fast. Think of the mind like a Polaroid camera. The picture develops quickly, but unless emulsion is used on the picture to stabilize it, the images can fade rapidly. In the learning process, the "emulsion" is to write as well as look at the information.

Visual learners can also have trouble with oral directions and may ask, "What are we supposed to do now?" right after the teacher has explained it. When this irritates the teacher or she says, "You weren't listening," anxiety builds in the student. The fact is, he probably was listening, but needs a visual or graphic representation of what the directions are—on the board or on a sheet on the desk—to do his best. Learning to read with an entirely phonetic-based approach proved frustrating and difficult for Josh. (Check chapter 7 for the best methods for visual students.) And unless he and other visual learners become really good note takers, they will tend to tune out class lectures and presentations.

Make sure your child has an eye exam by the age of three, because vision problems can cause learning problems in children. Nearsightedness; farsightedness; crossed eyes; and lazy eye, or amblyopia—the main reasons kids need glasses—can all affect reading and the ability to see the symbols and letters on the board. In first through third grade, 10 to 15 percent of children wear glasses, and in later grades, 20 percent. Most vision problems can be corrected and the child's learning not be adversely affected.

making the most of visual learning

Any time visual students can change or translate a chapter into a diagram, chart, or drawing, it will help them understand and retain what they read. Here are many ways to help visual learners capitalize on their strengths:

Outline and graphically represent ideas. All students need to develop good note-taking skills for classroom lectures and orally presented material. This is especially important for visual learners because just listening to someone talk tends to put them to sleep and brings on a major attack of boredom. To keep tuned in and learning, visual learners need to record and remember information.

Study cards. Kids can use three-by-five-inch or four-by-six-inch index cards in any subject. For example, in geography: Write the state on front and the capital on back (include a drawing if desired). In French or other foreign language: Write the French word on front, English equivalent on back. In history, science, or literature: Write the question on front, answer on back.

These study cards can also be used for a variety of purposes—note taking in class, textbook highlights, or for vocabulary and key words to learn for a test. They're handy because kids can slip them in their pocket and bring them out several times a day to read and review while waiting in line or if extra minutes remain in class.

Early elementary students can write each letter of the alphabet on index cards and draw an accompanying picture with felt-tip, colored pens. They can also write difficult words from the day's reading assignment on one side of the cards and illustrate them on the other side. After the words are written and illustrated, someone can go over them with the student orally (either at school or at home); if the student forgets a word, the student can refresh her memory by looking at the illustration on the flip side. This helps the student develop a mental picture for each word.

Index cards can also fit in a Ziplock bag and go in a backpack—perfect for "studying on the go." In addition, absorbing the amount of information on an index card is quicker and less overwhelming than studying everything on an 8 ½ by 11 inch sheet of paper. Get a different color of card for each class. A file box is an efficient way to store the study cards to prepare for the six-week, nine-week, or semester test.

Make mind maps. Also called learning maps, these pictorial representations of information are great ways to organize, learn, and remember, both in and out of the classroom. Since the mind map uses visual and verbal skills, and thus both sides of the brain, it boosts learning and memory. Constructing the map helps the student see and understand the connection between key ideas and increases comprehension of the material. Organized information is much easier to remember and retrieve at test time or a later date. Mind maps can be written on paper or on four-by-six-inch index cards.

The main topic goes in the middle and the related ideas on lines leading to the subtopics. The visually oriented student usually enjoys outlining the material in this way; it provides a visual cue to recall during study and test times, which is much better than several pages of expository information. After the student makes the map, he can discuss the information pictured with someone else—a study partner, small group, or parent, and review it each day leading up to the test. Then, the day before the exam, he can write the diagram on his whiteboard while explaining it to someone else.

Create illustrated time lines. For history, an illustrated time line is a good way to visually depict dates, events, and key ideas of a historical period. On a large sheet of paper or even larger sheet of butcher paper, have your child write the date, the name of the event, and under it, an illustration, symbol, or cartoon that represents it.

Write class notes. When notes need to be taken in a spiral notebook, a good way to record them is to have your child draw a straight line down the entire page to section off the right two-thirds. In the right section go notes from the board or teacher's lecture during class time. Then every night in the left or "recall" section, he reads over that day's class notes, summarizes the major concepts, and writes key words or adds a symbol or picture of the main ideas. On the left side of the notebook, he can write down a question that the teacher might ask on the material. To study, the student covers the right side, looks at the key words or symbols on the left, and sees what he can recall. This note-taking process helps integrate the concepts and connect ideas.

Utilize colored sticky notes. These are great little tools for keeping up with tasks and questions. They can be used as:

- Visual cues for remembering assignments. If the teacher assigns page 25, even-numbered problems 1–30, the student can put a sticky note on page 25 with the page numbers and instructions briefly written on the note. It helps to let the note stick out a little so when the student opens his locker to go home, he sees that the book needs to be taken home for an assignment.

- A harness for wandering thoughts. Keep at least ten blank notes adhered to the inside of every textbook, notebook, and assignment planner. If, in the middle of a class lecture the student finds her mind wandering (and if they're honest, most students easily admit to this), she can simply write that distracting thought on the sticky note and place it in her assignment planner. Once the note is written, she knows that she'll be able to tend to the idea later and can go back to concentrating on the lesson.

- Asking questions. Notes inside textbooks or spiral note-books can indicate a question the student needs to ask the teacher or a concept the student doesn't understand.

- Making lists. The sticky notes are good places to list things to do, and when stuck on the assignment note-book or desk, help the student get and stay organized.[2]

limit television viewing

Watchers tend to view more television than Doers or Talkers because they love the visual stimulation. As one mom I know said, "My auditory daughter Lauren watches a minimum of television because she'd rather be talking on the telephone, listening to music, or being with friends. My kinesthetic son is too busy riding his bike, jumping on the trampoline, or occupied with a project in the garage. But Jared, my little visual guy, will stare at the tube for hours! I can hardly get him away from it unless it's to play a video game."

Whether it's the visual candy of TV, video games, or computer screen, allow it only in moderation for your visually oriented child and provide projects, hobbies, activities, and books in his interests.

highlighting and color-coding

Another way for Watchers to focus on their strengths is highlighting key information that needs to be learned. (Highlighting is also helpful to kinesthetic students, because they're writing and busy with their hands). Often students will buy a colored highlighter and proceed to highlight everything on the page, which doesn't turn out to be very helpful in remembering key words or concepts. Instead, buy a variety of colored highlighters: pink, blue, yellow, orange, green. Then color-code the information.

Students can use this highlighting method when studying their notes or when reading textbooks if highlighting is allowed. For a history chapter, for example, key concepts are highlighted in yellow, answers to key chapter questions in pink, vocabulary words in green, and definitions in orange. In English, to facilitate identifying the parts of speech: green for nouns, blue for verbs, yellow for modifiers (adjectives and adverbs), and pink for connectives. In science, highlighting aids classification, vocabulary, and reading comprehension. And in math, the student can highlight the main points in word problems and the answer in another color.

Highlighting helps integrate the right- and left-hemisphere thinking skills because the color and patterns of coding appeal to the right (global) and the words and numbers to the left (analytic). Encourage your child, regardless of learning style, to try highlighting with color, and see it help him be more active, able to absorb more when reading, and retrieve it for tests.

computers

"My son learns best by putting spelling words or notes from science on his computer," said one mother. She calls out his spelling words orally, and he types them into the computer. "He then is able to see the information and concentrate on studying it." They have found he retains the information much better than when he reads or studies from a book.

Computers offer many possibilities for all learning styles, and visual students especially enjoy the stimulation. Composing and editing on a word-processing program facilitate writing skills. Drill and practice in math, spelling, vocabulary, and other subjects can be done with computer games and activities. Many children's books are in electronic format to be "read" on personal computers, with the added appeal of animated illustrations and sound effects. Although these shouldn't replace reading printed books to and with your child, they can be a creative addition to learning.

visual springboards

One of the best strategies to facilitate students' writing is mapping the story. I learned this at a teacher's workshop and have found it a terrific prewriting activity for young authors from first grade to college. It's not a new idea: Robert Louis Stevenson drew a watercolor map of an island to entertain his stepson on a rainy London day, and that map grew into his famous classic *Treasure Island*.

First, I draw a rough sketch or "map" of my own grade school on the board—or better, with bright markers on a large sheet of butcher paper taped up—and begin to relate the story of how I was injured and got my first stitches out on the asphalt playground and then my first black eye on the softball field. Each place where an incident happened, I put an X.

Then I have the students make a map of a place they remember: summer camp, Grandma's farm, the first house they remember living in. If it's a house, they draw the outline of the rooms. Then they put an X wherever an incident occurs to them. After completing their map, they rehearse the story orally by telling it to a partner.

After approximately ten minutes of storytelling (five for each person), the students begin to write the story on paper. Some of the most wonderful stories—by learners of all ability levels—are written because they have "seen" the story, "talked and heard" the story, and the ideas and sequence of events flow rapidly. These are later illustrated, edited, and published in a class anthology; posted on the walls of the hall or bulletin board; or sometimes even made into a collection of personal-experience stories in a book. The mapping activity can be done just as well at home to generate writing for a school or homeschool assignment.

A picture is another good way to stimulate writing. Give kids a selection of a few interesting pictures (from magazines) with characters and some action going on. They can choose one of the pictures and write a story about it.

Making a storyboard also jumpstarts the writing process. Give the student a long piece of paper and ask him to fold it into fours. Then he draws an illustration for the beginning of the story, two for the middle, and one for the end, before writing the story in words.

geography memory booster

Put a big, colorful map of the United States or world on a wall. When news reports highlight a city, state, or country, have your child note it on the map and put a small colored circle or push pin on it (which you can get at office-supply stores). Just seeing the map on a regular basis helps the student get an internal picture of the location of cities, states, rivers, and mountain ranges.

illustrating math problems

Visually representing story problems with real-life objects—pictures the child, parent, or teacher draws—aids understanding. Story problems can also be illustrated with magazine pictures by pasting a picture to a card containing the applicable story problem. In pairs, the children can figure out how to work the problem, and then they pass the picture on to the next pair to work.

When the teacher describes a triangle or rectangle and its characteristics, the visual student can try to picture the shape in her mind. When she can visualize the problem by making pictures or tallies of it on scratch paper as it is discussed, she'll be able to work it more quickly and correctly.

chore prompts

If chores at home and assignments at school are written down, children will do a 100 percent better job of following through and getting them done. Katy found this out by working with her ten-year-old son, Jacob. When she asked him orally to go get her school briefcase and turn off the computer (while she was tutoring a student), he forgot one or both instructions. But when later she handed him a yellow note with the two requests, he quickly went in, got her bag, turned off the computer, and delivered it, saying, "Anything else, Mom?" Often what we think is misbehavior is just misdirection. If you write down the instructions, and have your child cross them off as she completes them, you might be amazed at the cooperation.

enhancing visual skills for preschoolers and other learners

If your child is a preschooler or weak in Watcher skills, try these visual-memory boosting activities:

Memory tray. While your child is watching, place five objects on a tray one at a time, such as a comb, dollar bill, spoon, toy car, and pencil. Have her look at them closely for forty-five seconds. Then take the tray away and have your child close her eyes and see if she can "see" the objects and name them. Can she tell you the objects in the order they were placed on the tray? Can she name them in reverse order? Then put three of the same objects and one or two new ones on the tray and repeat the game. This is a great way to develop visual memory and recall.

Seeing and describing. Have your child look at something: an interesting picture, an object such as a bouquet of flowers or a toy you place on the table in front of her, or something you see as you are driving, like an animal or barn. Then have her close her eyes and describe it as vividly as possible; next, have her open her eyes and see how well she described the object.

Storytelling the visual way. Pick a familiar story, read it from a book (however many times is necessary), and then let your child practice telling it orally the way real storytellers do. First they picture it by scenes, creating a "mental movie" of the characters and action, scene by scene. Then have him tell the story, adding his own gestures, dialect, and even props.

Game playing. Visually oriented kids usually enjoy board games that develop visual discrimination skills and verbal skills at the same time. Games such as Cranium, Go to the Head of the Class, Monopoly, Scrabble, Connect Four, Chinese checkers, and others enable the child to have fun and yet learn and build skills at the same time. Card games build visual discrimination skills, visual memory, visual alertness, visual tracking (the ability to move the eyes smoothly to scan any plane and spot important details), eye-hand coordination, and many other important abilities children need for success in reading and math.[3]

Kids who discover how to best utilize their visual strengths enjoy learning more and grow in confidence. As you help enhance visual development in the ways suggested in this chapter, your child will grow to be observant and save valuable time. Improving the visual memory or "copier" in your child's brain will also help him excel in areas of interest—whether that is art, science, or another field.

If your child has two dominant strengths, like visual/ kinesthetic or visual/auditory, try combining these methods of study. Reinforce with a different learning strategy from the appropriate chapter, and then encourage your child to use the information in a creative, active way. In the next chapter, we'll look at how learning styles impact reading skills and how to make sure your child gets a solid foundation in reading.

how learning styles
impact reading skills

When Debra introduced the initial letter sounds to her six-year-old daughter Mary with the Spalding Phonics reading program, it just wasn't clicking. Mary couldn't remember the sounds and was distracted by the things going on in the room. Debra felt her daughter's strengths were visual and kinesthetic, so she decided to come up with her own multisensory approach to learning to read. Oh, the resourcefulness of a mom! She made a tape recording of the initial phonograms (or sounds) that the letters made. She then wrote the sounds in large letters on brightly colored cards. She taped the letter-sound cards in order all the way around the room, gave Mary a flashlight, and turned the light out in the room.

As the tape played and Mary heard it, she spoke the letter sound, traced around the letter with her flashlight, and then went on to the next card until she had gone all the way around the room. The activity kept Mary's attention; it was fun and it reinforced the auditory, visual, and kinesthetic modalities. On different days Mary traced the letters with glue and then sand and salt. As she mastered the initial sounds, they added new letter sounds until she had learned all seventy phonograms. With this creative method and some perseverance, everything clicked and Mary became an excellent reader.

Since reading is one of the most important challenges children face in the early grades, we as parents and teachers need to do everything we can to ensure their success. There is no perfectly right learn-to-read method that works for all children. But there are great resources today for helping kids with all kinds of learning differences become good readers. Although it is vitally important that children have intensive phonics training as the first building block in the reading process, we don't have to stick with one "program" and exclude all other approaches and modalities. In fact, an eclectic method that combines the best elements from several approaches may work well.

As was true for Mary, some children need extra help in the beginning stages of learning to read, such as individualizing the reading method by adding the component the child is strongest in. If the child is strong kinesthetically, it's important to add, in addition to phonics, hands-on practice such as tracing the letters in the air with the hand and whole arm and/or tracing the letters with a finger in sand or salt. If the connections between the sounds and the letters are not clicking for the visually oriented learner, use picture cues and focus on the shape of the letters, then write the letters or touch them. The auditory learner benefits by hearing a word first, having the phonetic sound pointed out, tracing or writing it, and then using it in a game or experience.[1]

If students are introduced to letters, words, and reading through their own learning style strength, they achieve much higher reading competency. Reading differences are common to all students, and if teachers and parents can know what their kids' strengths and differences are, they can help plan the best reading instruction for them.

Even if you're not the one teaching your child to read, your involvement can range from giving the teacher valuable information that can impact instruction, to volunteering to help in the classroom and encouraging reading at home. Sometimes it means homeschooling the child through the early years to ensure success in reading and basic skills. What's important is to intervene early so that a pattern of success, not failure, is established. Your involvement can make a huge difference to ensure a head start in reading.

Kathy, a Michigan mother, realized that the reading readiness of her third son, David, was just not where it should be before starting first grade. He had some attention problems and was behind where his two older brothers were at that stage. He hadn't progressed in decoding words and recognizing sounds by the end of the kindergarten year, and Mom became concerned he'd get behind. She decided to homeschool him for the first grade to give him the individual attention he needed to learn to read.

Besides his other instruction, every day for two or three hours he sat beside her so he could see the book while she read to him. During first semester she read aloud to him the entire LITTLE HOUSE ON THE PRAIRIE series, C. S. Lewis' CHRONICLES OF NARNIA books, and many other children's classics.

By the beginning of February, David took off reading to himself in first-grade level books, and within a month had moved up to third-

or fourth-grade level in his reading ability. The next year he entered school as a second grader who excelled and scored beyond grade level in reading. The head start his mom gave him made all the difference.

No child should be stuck with a "reading disabled" label because there are as many great methods to teach reading as there are different learning styles. Even if your child has some initial difficulties, you don't need to give up or lower your expectations. You can have his reading skills evaluated by a professional, start a home reading program that includes phonics and builds on your child's strengths (see list below), or get him an excellent tutor if needed—but make sure he learns to read well.

Here's a guide to some common reading methods for different kids, the learning styles they address, and practical things you can do to foster reading skills. To find these or other reading methods and materials, go to a search engine, type in "Phonics," "Visual Phonics," or whatever program you are seeking information on.[2]

phonics

Auditory-intensive phonics focuses on learning letters, blends, and syllable sounds. It moves from letter combinations to sentences, paragraphs, and stories. Different phonics programs include the Spalding Method; Sing, Spell, Read & Write; Zoo-Phonics; FrontLine Phonics; Hooked On Phonics; and others.

orten gillingham alphabetic phonics

Kinesthetic, tactile, auditory, visual; successfully used with dyslexic students.

A comprehensive, sequential, and structured form of phonics in which the student looks, says, and traces letters with fingers, and sounds are reinforced by all the senses.

visual phonics

Visual, auditory, kinesthetic, tactile.

A system of forty-six hand signs and written symbols to facilitate the development of speech and reading skills. Each written symbol is a visual representation of the hand sign. Visual Phonics can be used in conjunction with any good reading, literacy, or ESL (English as a Second Language) program.

whole language

Visual, auditory.

A literature-based reading and writing program that may not include phonics which was very popular in the 1980s but less prevalent today. Emphasis on the interrelationship of the language arts.

look-say, sight-word method

A rote word-memory system based on visual cues (mastering words by examining the nearby picture) and sight-word recognition.

motivating kids' reading by tapping into their style

Reading for Watchers. Visual learners of all ages—even adults—love books with beautiful, full-color illustrations. Young children who are strong visually tend to get up close to see the pictures and spend lots of time looking at books. Even at age one, our grand-daughter Josephine spent much focused time looking at her books and was fascinated by photos of family members, espe-cially photos of her daddy (who was deployed in the Pacific for four months).

Visual kids like wordless books, books like Richard Scarry's point-and-look books, books on how to draw things, and books with detailed photographs. John, a young boy we know, often scanned through the *World Book Encyclopedia* looking for a pic-ture that fascinated him; then he would stop to study it and read the accompanying article. Picture-literate people also like books with good descriptions of scenery and characters—it's easy for them to create a "mental movie" while reading.

Another effective way to motivate visual learners is let them watch the movie before reading the book. When a group of school children watched movies like *Anne of Green Gables, Raising the Titanic,* and *Black Beauty,* and National Geographic and Discovery Channel programs, all the books on those subjects quickly disap-peared from the school library.

Sparking auditory learners' reading. Language-oriented kids tend to love a good book. When young they especially love rhym-ing nursery tales, books with poetry, and rhythm or a singsong verse. They mimic the words of the refrain or interrupt your reading aloud to talk about the story. They enjoy hearing you tell stories and telling stories themselves. They're interested in books that have a lot of character development, good dialogue, and good plot. They often respond the best to phonics programs.

Books on tape or CD are great for kids with auditory/verbal strengths or those having difficulty with reading speed or comprehension. And since Talkers love discussions about what they're reading, they enjoy being in book clubs with their peers. The "Parents Sharing Books" program would be a great benefit to your child, and here's how it works: The parent gets a copy of the same book the child or teen is reading, and both read it independently but talk about the plot and characters or the ideas and opinions they have on the book. Hundreds of parents and kids around the country are sharing books and boosting comprehension and motivation for reading—and perhaps the biggest benefit is the connection and communication between parent and child.[3]

Motivating Doers' Reading Skills. Active kids enjoy active books. Young kinesthetic learners like pop-up books, scratch-and-sniff books, and books with movable parts. They'll often move around and do what the book says—if it's hop, jump, or run, they do it. Later they are drawn to adventure stories, science fiction, action stories, sports heroes' biographies, and books about certain sports. They read best when propelled by something they want to do (like a manual telling how to put together a go-cart or rocket).

Building on their natural interests is a secret to boosting all children's motivation for reading. "I was a terrible reader in elementary school," said William Jackson, one of the top marine biologists in the United States. "Until in the sixth grade, my aunt who lived in Japan sent me *The Omnibus of Science Fiction*. It was a huge volume with sixty stories about space adventures, scientists' accidents, and the creation of new life forms that ignited my imagination and stirred up my love of science." Jackson read it three or four times, and then went on to read Westerns, mysteries, and spy novels. That book opened a whole new world for him, and Jackson became a prodigious reader. He later pursued a career in marine biology and became director of the National Marine Fisheries Service in Galveston, Texas.

As Karen Gale, a reading specialist who has taught hundreds of children and adults to read, says, "The first thing I do is find out what the student is interested in." Besides the combination of phonics, visual cues, cluster method, and other approaches she uses to find what the child is picking up quickest and what makes the lightbulb go on (that is, makes reading happen), she asks what the child's very favorite things to learn about are. If the child is interested in topography, she uses books with pictures of volcanoes, from which the child sounds out words about volcanoes. When the student is ready, she has him write about volcanoes. Tapping into the child's center of learning excitement and what is most fascinating to him is a key to unlocking his reading potential.

Brian Campbell's mom was told he'd never learn to read because of his Williams Syndrome condition that causes retardation. But by using his love of car-wash words, she taught him to read, and he became not only an avid reader of many genres of books, but a knowledgeable, popular speaker at car wash owner's conventions around the country.

As you adapt reading methods and materials to your child's learning style, read aloud to her at home, and encourage daily independent reading in her favorite areas of interest, you'll go a long way toward helping her become a fluent, lifelong reader and a more successful student.

discovering your child's talents and gifts

By eleven years old, a young California artist named Alexandra had already created more than 350 paintings, some selling for as much as $125,000. She had discovered her love of creating art at age two while coloring and painting.

Elizabeth, an eight-year-old New Yorker I met, had an extensive repertoire on the violin and was invited to play at Carnegie Hall. At three, when she had started Suzuki violin lessons, she mastered the entire first book in two months. She sings all the time and can play anything she hears.

Elizabeth and Alexandra's experience illustrates that many talents show up early in life. Each child is unique, with a one-of-a-kind brain, special gifts and talents, and different ways of looking at life. Even kids who seem to have disabilities or struggle academically are gifted in some way. At age ten, Leslie wasn't placed in the "gifted" class at school because the teacher said her IQ was 100 instead of the required 125. Test taking was always a struggle for her and she graduated in the bottom of her law school class, but because of her people smarts, she beat out tough competition for a terrific paying job as an attorney and became very successful.

If we are astute observers of our kids, there are lots of clues to their talents. Even their memories and what they recall the best is a clue to potential talent. Musically talented people have an amazing ability to remember songs and musical patterns; the body-smart dancer has the muscle memory to recall intricate dance steps. The child with spatial talent remembers the route to a campsite better than anyone else in the hiking group, and the language-talented person remembers words the best and therefore memorizes a poem or speech with ease.

When a person understands his strengths and weaknesses and develops his talents, there's no telling what that person can achieve. Take Quincy Jones, for example. With his visual and musical talent, creativity comes naturally to this renowned composer, producer, publisher, and winner of dozens of Grammy and other awards. When he's composing, he sees pictures. When he sees pictures, he hears music. The ideas keep generating, and he finds himself writing in taxis or on airplanes, using menus, gum wrappers—anything that's handy—to capture ideas when the creativity is flowing. He can see and hear all the parts and pieces of a work in his head. But he admits he has limitations too. He has never learned to drive a car!

Auditory people tend to express their creativity through words and may become successful lawyers, writers, teachers, or radio or television broadcasters. People with visual and spatial talent conceptualize with ease; they think in pictures and diagrams. Engineers and artists share this ability; they see the painting or building before it's ever constructed. Like

Anne Geddes, the photographer who takes pictures of babies as angels, ladybugs, and even sleepy little birds. Whenever she sees an image of something in her mind, she sees a baby in it.

Maggie, a ballet and modern-dance teacher, said, "When I hear music or poetry, I think flowing shapes and see movement." Kinesthetically gifted people like Maggie learn and express themselves best through movement. They may become world-class athletes, actors, dancers, computer experts, or sculptors.

Just as these people found, learning differences are not just liabilities, as we tend to think of them. They are pathways to the great potential that lies within.

creative kids: problems or prodigies?

Talented kids may find school a discouraging place. Dean was an immensely creative child from an early age. He had a vivid, active imagination and a wonderful sense of humor. Along with the ability to be logical and conceptual, he loved music, reading, and writing creatively. In the classroom his approach to learning was so rapid (he learned most material in a few minutes) that he would then daydream, draw, or play with the kids next to him. This created some discipline problems.

"I found very few teachers who knew how to channel his boundless energy," said his mom, Sandy. Even fewer capitalized on his creativity instead of criticizing it.

In his home environment, his parents continued to encourage Dean to pursue projects and musical instruments with enthusiasm. But he began to hate school more and more. "If he'd only apply himself . . ." his parents often heard. They tried everything when low report cards came home—scolding, grounding. Nothing worked. The problem was, Dean didn't know how to involve his strengths in the learning process, and his talent and creativity were, for the most part, not recognized or developed at school.

One insightful teacher told Dean's parents he had an enormous personality, but it would take time for him to grow into it. By eighteen or nineteen he had! Although he barely graduated from high school, he became an A college student. As a music major, he mastered tuba, trombone, baritone, and guitar. He sang, composed music, and excelled in math and any class that required conceptual thinking—and has become a successful adult who worked as a professional musician and taught music. Told by a teacher in the early grades that he needed drugs to settle down his alleged hyperactivity (his parents declined), Dean is a calm guy with tremendous energy for creating and for weekend woodworking projects, but he balances his activity with quiet, reflective times.

a school's eye view of intelligence

Society and most schools don't always encourage creative thinkers like Dean. Test smarts, logical-math, and language abilities get kids high marks. At the elementary level, behavior, social skills, clerical abilities (skill with pencil and paper), and conformity is rewarded more than knowledge. Highly creative elementary children often become school problems. At the junior high and high school level, teachers emphasize verbal skills. And at the college level, problem-solving skills are emphasized.[1]

If your child has the "school's eye view of intelligence"— whatever that happens to be at her particular grade level and classroom—she's affirmed by good grades and recognized at awards assemblies. But kids whose strengths don't fit in the school system wonder about their worth and often experience frustration in the classroom.

As Robert Sternberg, Yale professor and researcher, said, "The school's eye view of intelligence" plays "a major role in determining who succeeds and who fails, not only in school, but also in later life."[2] Students who have creative abilities or practical, real-life intelligence "may come to perceive themselves as not particularly smart because of their lesser test scores and the lesser reinforcement they receive in school."[3] He says they are at risk for seeing themselves as impostors, people who succeed even though they aren't very capable or don't deserve to succeed.

Although intelligence tests and standardized, pencil-and-paper tests are poor measuring devices of real talent, that's what most schools use to identify kids' abilities. Sternberg himself did terribly on IQ tests in elementary school. "In elementary school I had severe test anxiety," he said. "I'd hear other people starting to turn the page, and I'd still be on the second item. I'd utterly freeze." In sixth grade, he did so poorly on an IQ test that he was sent to retake it with the fifth graders. But by seventh grade he was designing and administering his own test of mental ability as part of an original science project. In tenth grade he studied how distractions affect people taking mental-ability tests. A professor at Yale University, he has written hundreds of articles and several books on intelligence, and he received numerous fellowships and awards for his research and his "Triarchic Theory" of intelligence.[4]

discovering talent

It's up to us as parents to recognize, develop, and appreciate our children's intelligence gifts and talents instead of depending on the school to do it. Whether it be creative, analytical, or practical intelligence—focus on what your child does best and success will follow. Self-worth and motivation will grow. Success in one area helps kids develop the momentum to work harder in tasks that are more difficult.

Research at Gallup, Inc., an international research firm that studied more than 250,000 successful professionals in various fields, showed that the highest levels of achievement come when people are matched with activities that use their strengths. This study suggests that, instead of spending the majority of our time trying to correct weaknesses and remedy problem areas, we should focus on our special talents.

"We estimate that for every one strength," wrote Donald Clifton and Paula Nelson, authors of *Soar with Your Strengths,* "we possess roughly one thousand nonstrengths. That ratio shows it would be a huge waste of energy to try to fix all of our weaknesses."[5]

how to discover talents

By finding something your child is good at and then investing in that skill, you can avoid what Dr. Mel Levine describes as the "chronic success deprivation" in which a student goes through many years of life with few, if any, real triumphs and has little chance to develop her gifts. "A kid who is not very popular, who has school problems, and who doesn't play sports well may be deprived of success in life at that point. Sometimes a student like that just gives up or gets very depressed."[6]

You know your child the best, love her the most, and can spot talent and intelligence that school overlooks. All kids are born with a lot of potential in one or several areas (even those with disabilities) and several areas of talent usually work together in concert as kids grow up and use them in a career. For example, a NASA engineer would possess spatial talent, math, and analytical intelligence. A politician might be linguistically and logically intelligent and have strong people skills. Succeeding as a professional dancer and instructor requires body, musical, and interpersonal smarts.[7] But the determinant factor in whether or not the young person's talent blooms is the support, encouragement, and development offered by parents.

Here are some ways to begin:

Observe your child as he works, plays, interacts with people, solves problems, and does homework.

Listen. Ask questions and you'll discover what sparks her, whether at school or at home. Ask: What do you like to do most of all? What are you good at? What do you enjoy doing at school? Find her center of learning excitement, the subjects she is most fascinated with and wants to learn more about. Observe what she takes the most pride in. The answers are a clue to abilities and strengths you can help her develop.

Be aware of character and personal strengths—such as empathy, which is needed by nurses, physical therapists, and others in the caring professions; or nurturing abilities, which can help make great teachers, parents, and managers; or perception, which novel writers and artists possess.

Take another look at what we often think of as "negative qualities" in our children. With an eye to the possibilities, you can see their strengths through these: The "daydreamer" may be a creative thinker or an inventor. The bossy child often has administrative ability that can put her in charge of her own company someday. The student who balks at directions and finds out-of-the-box ways to do things might be a creative thinker. The confident kid who is always challenging your opinions may have valuable logical and analytical ability when she "grows into" her gift. In the meantime, be patient and remind yourself that your child will grow into her gift as she matures.

Get a bigger picture of smart. Since having a narrow view of intelligence keeps us from recognizing the abilities of the children around us, we're going to look at descriptions of several different talents in the next chapter and then what you can do to develop these strengths in your child. I've combined two—Robert Sternberg's and Howard Gardner's model of intelligence—to help you gain a broader perspective of what's smart and thus find the "hidden treasures" in your child.

And even if you don't think your child has a gift of creative thinking (or another area of intelligence) but want to encourage those skills, you can use the suggestions to help his or her development in that area.

developing your child's talents and gifts

Once there was a boy who never adjusted contentedly to school. He was not a good all-around student, hated tests and exams, and did not make high grades. He had no school friends, and his speech was delayed. Some teachers found him a problem and described him as dull. His father was ashamed of his lack of athletic ability. But he was insatiably curious, loved to explore ideas, and had an incredible focus on his own little projects. Who was he? The theoretical physicist and Nobel prize winner Albert Einstein, whose curiosity and perpetual sense of wonder lasted his whole life.[1]

Since kids are always growing and new skills emerging, not all the talent kids have will emerge in their early life or be recognized by others, but there are inborn gifts that can give them purpose, joy, and direction. And the clues to these talents are often there from youth. Only two of the kinds of intelligence described below are easily identified on standardized tests and praised at school.

Here are seven ways kids are smart or gifted, and how to help your child's talents grow:

creative thinkers

"Academic smarts are easy to find, but creativity is rare and pre-cious," says Robert Sternberg.[2] He described his graduate stu-dent Barbara, who had lots of creative thinking ability, wanted to make her own rules, and be given a lot of freedom. Whether the assignment was a science project or a speech she had to give in high school, she went at the task in an innovative, fresh way. She didn't make the best test scores in the class, but had great ideas and was a very creative thinker. She's a "big picture" person who looks at the whole concept rather than the details. She also had what's called "synthetic ability": the insight to combine different experiences or ideas and see them in a new way, or the ability to look at an old problem and come up with new solutions.[3] Barbara is a classic example of the creative thinker.

When studying literature, creative kids would prefer to make up their own story with an original plot and characters rather than analyze what various critics said about a given work. They may score only in the average range in high school or college, but in graduate school or in their career, their ability to create new ideas and implement them causes them to soar in achievement.

how can we enhance creative ability?
Encourage creative kids to undertake projects, such as creating original computer programs, doing science experiments, creating art projects, writing and illustrating their own books—whether they relate to school or not. Whatever their interests are, let them

do creative work in those areas and help them find fascinating projects to do on their own. Saying "Try it; see what happens" or "That's a great idea!" can be a great encouragement to the creative thinker.

Save the raw materials of creation—odds and ends of stuff can be made into something else, a hodgepodge sculpture or an invention—and give your child time to explore and experiment. Gib, a creative guy who was insatiably curious about how things worked, was provided with many objects to take apart in the garage: small engines, a toaster, a coffeepot, even an old car. He finally progressed to putting them back together and fixing them.

Help your child set up a center for creative activity. Whether for artwork, building rockets or woodworking, for dismantling and fixing old toasters or other machinery, or other creative pursuits, this should be a place where your child can make a mess if it's part of the process. Don't expect kids to be perfectly neat and tidy while creating. Stock the creative center with Styrofoam packing, boxes, wood scraps, yarn, nails, buttons, seashells, pipe cleaners, and colored construction paper, in addition to paint, glue, clay, and typical art supplies.

Encourage questions. Creative thinkers ask extraordinary questions: How does the heart work? How was that metal sculpture built? Encourage them! If one of your child's questions boggles your mind, respond, "That's a great question, but I don't know the answer!" Write it down on an index card, and next time you're at the library together, search for the answer. Or search for answers on the Internet. Some questions don't have one "right" answer; let your child think in an open-ended way about possibilities.

Take interesting outings to art galleries and hands-on science museums, to see a research scientist work in his lab, or to watch a potter or other craftsperson at work. Cultivate whatever area your child expresses an interest in. And don't limit creativity to just the artistic fields—a person can be creative in music or computers, in science and research, in problem solving, in writing, dance, or in a host of other pursuits. Wherever your child's creativity shows itself, encourage it.

analytical and logical talent

Analytical students tend to be task-oriented and like following rules and procedures. Travis is a whiz at test taking and scores high on standardized tests. Multiple-choice questions are his favorite. His analytical, critical thinking has catapulted him to the top of his math and science classes. He's a detail person who thrives on solving complicated theorems in geometry, and he scored high on the SAT for college entrance. Analytical skills like Travis's are valuable in business and industry, teaching and research, psychology and social issues, and math and science fields, to name just a few.

Kids with logical and analytical talent tend to be fascinated with numbers, order, sequencing, and counting. They may be excellent problem solvers but weak in social skills. The analytical child's questioning of everything will not necessarily make him the "student of the month." Parents and teachers may sometimes want to turn off his searching (and sometimes irritating) questions.

As a child, Tom Lough was frustrated in science and math courses. It was tough for teachers to make the material interesting and challenging enough, and he consistently asked questions they couldn't answer. He was curious about everything from the origin of the constellations to how a muscle works. School science was taught by rote and included few experiments. Although he wasn't challenged in school, his interest in science continued to grow from reading encyclopedias at home and going on outings with his dad, an amateur astronomer, to watch meteor showers and view constellations. He entered a science fair competition with a three-dimensional model of his personal theory on how the planets were formed and took honorable mention.

Tom went on to get a bachelor's degree in engineering from West Point, a master's in geodetic science, a master's in physics, a doctorate in educational psychology, and is now a physics professor. His parents' encouragement of his analytical/logical gifting made all the difference.

how can we encourage analytical skills?

Emphasize analysis in parent-child interactions. When you interact with your children, give them reasons for what you're doing and encourage them to provide reasons for what they do. You can discuss and analyze politics, social issues, and things going on in their school, community, and lives on a regular basis. Talking with your children about why something happens and what they think about it encourages analytical thinking. Analyzing world events after you have watched the news together stimulates this kind of critical thinking.

Provide measuring tools and give your child problems to solve. A ruler, a compass, a map, a calculator, an egg timer, balance scales, thermometers, and a stopwatch are a good start. Ask questions such as: How much new carpet will it take to cover the living room floor? How can you find out if your new bookshelf will fit through the door into your room? How long will it take us to get to Grandma's at a speed of fifty-five miles per hour?

Provide opportunities to conduct real experiments and hands-on science projects, whether it's identifying constellations with a star map or collecting and labeling insects and butterflies. Even in your kitchen you can stimulate curiosity by asking questions such as: What happens to water when it boils? What happens when cream is shaken hard? Why does the banana decompose after many days on the kitchen counter?

Encourage collections of rocks, stamps, coins, insects, shells, or other materials. Provide a shelf or plastic box with dividers for the collection. Analytical kids love to classify and categorize, and collections provide a great opportunity to use these skills.

Provide computer games that use strategy and focus on problem solving and games like Mastermind, Battleship, chess, and math puzzle books.

Accelerate math progress. If your child is advanced in math and thus bored with the level of math at school, challenge him outside of class. When sixth grader Philip was doing well on his math exams but failing math because he skipped the homework he found boring, his mother hired a college student to teach him algebra, but persuaded him to do his homework to keep his teacher happy. There are also many summer math and science enrichment programs for children gifted in this area at colleges and universities around the country.

musical talent

A good clue to a musically gifted child is perfect pitch at a very early age.[4] The musically intelligent child can also imitate tone, rhythm, and melody, and thus remember and sing songs from hearing them once or twice. Although all children have some musical aptitude, this child has what we call a high music IQ. Our daughter Alison loved music from a very early age and had near perfect pitch and an ear for dialects, lyrics, and melodies. She grew up singing and started piano lessons at age six. In junior high she began playing the guitar and helping lead worship in youth group. She's composed songs and sung on commercially produced CDs and, although she's a busy mother of two little boys, sings at weddings and continues to use her musical talent when opportunities open up.

ways to encourage your musically gifted child

Sing to him and play a variety of good music at home and in the car, including classical music, folk music, traditional children's music, and the best Broadway scores and movie sound tracks.

If your child consistently has an interest in music, rent a piano, buy a flute or other instrument, find a compatible teacher, and try summer music camps for enrichment.

Tap into computer composing. If you have a home computer, a software program that allows your child to write and perform original music is a great resource. With one program, Songwriter, the child can experiment with time and melody to create single-voice compositions. With others, the child can print out the score of an original song.

Take your child to symphony concerts, live musical theater, and other musical events in your community. Live musical concerts are often where kids get the inspiration to play a particular instrument or get remotivated if they're in a "slump" with their lessons.

Provide opportunities to perform. Piano or violin recitals are great but may come only once a year. Give your child chances to enjoy performing by playing his instrument or singing at nursing homes or charity and church events. When you're picking a new school, find one that has an excellent music program where your child will have the fun of practicing and performing with a group of his peers on a regular basis.

practical and people smarts

One aspect of intelligence Sternberg has identified is what he calls "everyday" or practical intelligence, the ability to know what's required and to go ahead and do it right. This common-sense ability reminds me of a junior high student I had named Kim who was "street smart" in the sense of having a lot of practical, usable intelligence. She was a hard worker who knew how to play the game—whether that game was classroom competition, how to get into the best college, or how to deal with people on her part-time job for a radio station. She made sure her activities contributed to a great application for the school she wanted acceptance to. She ran for student government and won.

Kim has learned how to take her abilities and skills and apply them to the everyday tasks and problems of life. And she knows how to jump over obstacles. She knows how to talk with men and women of all ages, understand their feelings, and lead in a group (we call this "people smart"). Her enthusiasm is contagious: in school she was skilled at getting other kids to join in her projects. Kim made acceptable grades, but not top grades; however, she came out on top because of her common sense and her ability to adapt to whatever environment she finds herself in.[5]

how can we encourage practical and people smarts?

Get kids to interact with people. Part-time jobs, service projects, and full-time summer jobs when they're old enough are great ways to help children develop this ability. For example, we encouraged our son to work in a lawyer's office in the summer where he had to deal with people and be cooperative and interdependent with the staff. Whether it's as an assistant to a vet or being a candy striper hospital volunteer, work experiences offer terrific opportunities to develop practical intelligence.

Giving kids leadership opportunities at home and church or

neighborhood help develop people skills. For example, put him in charge of a project within his ability level, like planning his own birthday party or coordinating the family campout or a fund-raising project for a charity you're involved with.

Give your child chores at home, because chores are "real-world stuff" that develop responsibility, adaptability, and the skill of doing things on time. Also, suggest she start a business in her own back (or front) yard like dog sitting, car washing, catering, lawn mowing, or something that uses her expertise or talent.

Show your child negotiating skills for resolving conflict with friends and family members. Instead of settling sibling arguments for your kids, help them find their own solutions. "I see you're having trouble sharing Lego building blocks. Why don't you work out a plan? You could use this timer to have individual turns with the blocks and chart your schedule, cooperate and build something together, or you could think of another idea."

Direct your child toward a good organization like Scouts, 4-H, or a church youth group where he can learn the dynamics of group activities and work with different kinds of people toward common goals.

Encourage independent work. When she has a history project or report to write, help her make a list of what is necessary to get it done on time and a timetable or calendar to divide the task into doable bites. Brainstorm to generate ideas and show her how to research on the Internet or at the library for books and materials, but encourage her to work independently after you get her started rather than waiting until the last night and doing it for her.

visually talented kids

Spatial or visual ability means being able to visualize an object in your mind's eye and imagine how it would look if it were turned around. Children who are spatially gifted are great at visualizing pictures, objects, and even how things work in their mind. These children can find their way around a city, a ski area, or a large, multifloored building with ease. They notice intricate details, and can see something once and reproduce it on paper—and thus possess artistic or design ability.[6] These superb visualizers may love drawing, sculpting, assembling complicated puzzles, photography, or graphic design depending on their interests.

Brian Jones, a young man born deaf, doesn't need to hear to create three-dimensional models of buildings for large companies. He has excellent spatial talent, three-dimensional conception, and a sharp attention to detail. Despite being hearing-impaired, he is pursuing a successful career in drafting. Even as a child he noticed models of buildings in magazines and on trips to downtown and paid careful attention to the structure. Like many spatially talented people, he has a vivid imagination. Brian's future looks bright because he has found a career area that focuses on his strength. Spatially gifted people can become architects, sculptors, artists, or design engineers.

ways to develop spatial and visual talent

Provide markers, paper, charcoal, brushes, a good pair of scissors, modeling plastics, an easel, and other art materials. Unusual art supplies for crafts such as origami, the Japanese art of paper folding, are helpful. Origami is a wonderful way to learn about the many possible relationships between different shapes. Children can make birds, giraffes, boats, or party hats out of the origami paper (instruction books with colorful paper are available at children's bookstores and craft shops). Lessons in pottery making or drawing could be helpful.

Provide games like checkers, chess, and three-dimensional tic-tac-toe and computer graphics programs like Paintbrush or Picturewriter that stretch visual abilities.

Try tangrams, two-dimensional geometric pieces (such as squares, triangles, rectangles) that can be arranged to make formations and shapes like animals or houses or to fit in a tangram puzzle book. Spatially talented kids love the challenge of tangram puzzles.

Encourage projects like assembling models of airplanes or rockets, or inventing things. Most important, follow your child's interests, whether that is drawing milk cartons in perspective, making paper airplanes, or painting murals.

Go on walks in new, unfamiliar terrain and encourage your visualizer to draw maps of where he's been.

body-smart kids

Children with physical talent can coordinate muscle movements, operate with grace and timing, and use their body and other objects with skill and precision. These children are usually standouts in athletics, drama, mechanics technology, or any hands-on endeavor. Their brain coordinates their movements and abundant energy with a grace that may be evident at an early age.

What some kinesthetically talented people possess is in the small motor rather than large motor area. Paul could drive a car from an early age, and years before he was old enough, longed for his pilot's license. Very coordinated in sports, he can't repair the family dishwasher or plumbing, but after only a few pilot's lessons he could fly an airplane with skill. At one point, his instructor covered up the dials and said, "Fly this plane at an airspeed of exactly eighty miles per hour." Without any difficulty, Paul was able to feel how fast he was going, fly the plane by instruments, and when his instructor took the clipboard off the dial, he was exactly on the correct speed.

This ability to "feel," plus dexterity and coordination, make kinesthetically intelligent people excellent actors, dancers, professional baseball pitchers, computer technicians, and sometimes, brain surgeons.

enhancing body smarts and skills

Give your child opportunities to explore different sports to find one that she can enjoy or excel in. Consider team sports like soccer, basketball, or hockey, or individual ones like gymnastics, tennis, or cross-country running. What's important is finding a physical activity your child enjoys and developing skills in that area.

Provide things to take apart and a toolbox with pliers, screwdriver, hammer, and wrench. Old clocks and electric toys found at garage sales are fun to dissect and "fix." Your child may eventually be able to repair your television or other household machines like my friend's kinesthetically talented son Chase (they've made some great savings on repair bills). An erector set and electronic gadgets, woodworking tools in the garage, trees to climb, or a dart board on the wall are all good outlets for kinesthetic talent.

Provide opportunities to see and participate in a variety of athletic events in the community, from dance recitals to swim meets, from being a member of the YMCA or sports clubs, to participating in horseback-riding competitions and Olympic festivals.

Find mentors. If your child is interested in veterinary medicine and you know nothing about it, see if there's a local vet she could work for on Saturdays. If your son is fascinated with marine biology, look for a summer program at the beach on the subject. If making movies is the interest, put a video camera in her hand to film family and school events. The more real-life opportunities they have to try things out and explore their interests, the more motivated these kids will be and the sooner they'll find their niche.

language-talented kids

Language-talented children talk early and are fascinated with the sound and meaning of words. Their parents may even find themselves thinking, "If only he'd stop talking!" Linguistically gifted kids express their verbal ability by telling descriptive stories, memorizing commercials word for word, picking up foreign phases easily, and enjoying wordplay like tongue twisters and puns. Generally, these children love reading and being read to, may teach themselves to read, and rapidly build a large vocabulary.

Ann excelled in language arts throughout elementary school and took all the honors and advanced placement courses offered in English and history in high school. A prodigious reader, she tested out of two years of college English because of her own at-home reading of the classics, in addition to her honors courses. Although quiet, she loved to write, and became the editor of her college newspaper, entered law school at twenty, and plans to work as a political journalist for a large city newspaper. Although she was frustrated with math, and has a hard time finding her way around a new city, she's a whiz with words, creative in her expression, and loves the challenge of a new article to research.

ways to encourage language-talented kids

Read to them daily and get their own library card. Provide lots of books and look for other language outlets like pinning poems on the refrigerator, doing crossword puzzles, or memorizing poems together. Talk about books you're reading at dinnertime, and introduce a foreign language through music tapes in that language, which you can listen to in the car on errands or to and from school.

Make books and value written expression. From the stories your preschooler dictates to you, to longer fantasies and tales your school-age child writes, value your child's expression. Encourage her to make personal greeting cards, to write a family newsletter, to write scripts for plays and perform them with friends.

Find opportunities to develop speaking abilities, such as joining Toastmasters with your child or taking an enrichment speech course at a local college or being on the debate team at school.

Encourage journaling. For a birthday or Christmas, buy a blank book and have your child write down ideas, poems, travel experiences, and stories in a journal. Journal keeping is excellent practice for developing language talent.

Have fun with language. Make up rhymes, limericks, and tongue twisters, and introduce wonderful classics like *Winnie the Pooh, The Wizard of Oz,* and C. S. Lewis's *Chronicles of Narnia*—and read aloud as a family. Provide recorded books for car trips and place books by your child's bed to read at bedtime.

If your child writes a promising poem or story, help her submit it to a children's or teen magazine for possible publication. There are many young people's magazines that publish children's writing. Publishing means sharing and there are many ways kids can share their writing—at school, in a neighborhood newspaper, or family round-robin newsletter, in the local paper, or on websites that publish children's writing.

winning with strengths

There's a temptation to have our kids involved in a myriad of activities. To help capitalize on your child's strengths, pick one or two areas at a time she'd enjoy pursuing or is passionate about (instead of involving your child in a dozen lessons, athletic training programs, teams, and hobbies) and go with that for a while to see where it leads. From studies in the 1920s of over 1,440 highly gifted children, some who accomplished things in life and some who didn't, the research concluded that "what distinguished those of spectacular achievement from low achievement and failure was prudence and forethought, willpower, perseverance and desire. They chose among their many talents and concentrated their efforts."[7]

The development of these intelligences may be more important than some of the issues we put so much emphasis on during the school years. Yes, classwork is important, good grades are important, and high standardized test scores make parents proud. But research shows that IQ and other standardized tests are poor predictors of achievement in life. They can predict school performance itself, but not what the children are going to accomplish in the real world.

As you nurture your child's hidden talent, he will grow in confidence and purpose. He will develop motivation to tackle tougher assignments at school and beyond. Later you can help your child develop goals and focus on what he wants to do in summer vacations, after-school activities, in later education, and in life. Those "hidden talents" can become a great source of joy and direction.

handling weaknesses so they don't block strengths

Whaat are your child's weaknesses and how do these operate in the classroom? How does the teacher teach and in what ways can we bypass weaknesses? These are two important questions that have a large bearing on preventing problems and keeping kids on track for learning.

Keisha, a ninth grader, was having trouble passing science class, so her mother found a tutor to help her. But her greater problem was the migraine headaches she experienced each day at school that the doctor attributed to "stress." In fact, these severe headaches had caused her to miss thirteen days of the nine weeks and adversely affected her grades. Her mother had tried to help, but was frustrated with her daughter's failing science test scores and was after her every night to study harder.

After some evaluation and dialogue with Keisha, the tutor began to see the underlying problem. Every day in science class the students had to take notes while the teacher rapidly talked and lectured while scribbling notes on the board. When Keisha had to listen and try to follow the lecture, while writing notes from the board, trying to spell correctly, and remember all at the same time, the fuses blew; she became frustrated and overwhelmed, and a migraine often resulted.

Since the notes were necessary to succeeding in the class, parent, tutor, and teacher worked out an alternative plan: The teacher had Keisha listen while he lectured and wrote on the board. She could listen much better when not writing, as the auditory pathway was her strength. Then she was permitted to hand-copy another student's notes after class. That afternoon, when she went home to study, Keisha read her notes into a tape recorder and played them back later to review. She began making Bs and Cs instead of Fs, and best of all, didn't miss any school that grading period due to migraines.

Dr. Mel Levine likens this kind of accommodation or strategy that bypasses a student's weakness as a detour we take when construction blocks a highway. Kids may need alternative routes like these, he says, so they can go where they need to and learn what is required while working on the basic problem (like memory or reading skills, for example). The bypass method can prevent a breakdown or humiliation in the classroom because of a learning weakness.[1] But he also encourages that when arrangements are made to bypass, the student be asked for a "payback"—some kind of additional work that helps them sustain their pride and is fair to other students who don't get an adaptation.[2]

how teachers teach

It also helps to understand that a teacher's instructional style can have a major effect on how your child performs in the classroom.

The way teachers teach tends to emerge right out of our own learning style—especially under time pressure when there's a lot of material to get across. Some teachers prefer a quiet environment in the classroom and assign a lot of silent reading. Some do lots of hands-on experiments and projects. Others do an abundance of talking and explaining to get concepts across to their class.

These styles interact with kids' weaknesses and learning styles. A surefire way to stifle learning for the visual student is to say everything aloud, rapidly, and not to write any information on the board. For the auditory student, saying "Shhh!," having a no-talking-while-learning rule, prohibiting questions, and mandating that all reading be silent can produce problems. For the Doer child, saying "Be still! No moving! Stay in your seat!" and "Stop drumming your fingers!" combined with all pencil-and-paper assignments and little or no hands-on activity is a sure deterrent to learning. When your child has a teacher whose teaching style is just the opposite of his way of receiving information, the combination can have a negative impact on school performance. Let's look at some teaching style patterns below:

Talker teachers explain a great deal, encourage class discussions, and frequently ask for feedback. They may have a plainer classroom but one that is more functional than attractive. They like team-teaching. They may encourage students to study together or participate in small discussion groups. This teacher usually gives instructions for assignments orally rather than in written form, which is fine as long as your child also has auditory strengths; otherwise he may not get all the directions.

When there is assigned reading, it's talked about in class afterward. When literature or history is studied, it would be natural for this teacher to have students tape or video-record "on-the-scene" interviews with characters. Guest speakers may be brought in. This teacher likes to call out questions on a pop quiz and have students write down the answers. This approach wouldn't bring out the best in the visual learners and the long lectures and discussions might put the Doers to sleep (or encourage them into flicking pens and acting out). It takes extra efforts for her to create visual accompaniments to lessons or provide hands-on experiences, but it's important especially since many of her students will need them to comprehend the material.

Visually oriented teachers (Watchers) put up lots of colorful bulletin boards and displays, even in upper grades. There are learning centers highlighted by attention-getting artwork. At open house, this teacher's classroom is a big hit. They tend to use a variety of visual teaching materials such as written handouts, Powerpoint presentations, videos, and a class Web page. As a parent, you can see he put a lot of time and effort into making a creative physical environment for the students. (One social studies teacher's room I sat in during my son's high school open house had so many pictures of people they were studying, posters of historical events, a huge time line, and other visuals covering the walls that I couldn't concentrate on what she was saying.)

The visual teacher has the schedule for the day and directions written on the board and may not provide a great deal of oral explanation (and may quickly grow weary of answering a curious student's oral questions). Reading is frequently done silently; reports written and illustrated by students are backed with construction paper and displayed neatly in the hall.

Doer/Mover teachers usually have a classroom that reflects their interactive, hands-on teaching style. Judy, a fourth-grade teacher I knew, had on one wall a huge picture of a clown named Willy, juggling yellow, pink, and orange fluorescent balls with the students' names in cursive. A large banner on the west wall said "Kids Are Special." Another bulletin board has a large turkey the children helped make. Each child took a paper feather off the bird, wrote on it the name of someone he was thankful for, and put it back on the turkey's wings and tail. Another board has photos and a newspaper article of the teacher's clown-camp experience.

Desks were in the middle of the room in rows, but moved often so the class could do a lot of floor work and group work. Before Judy introduced multiplication to the class, she realized they were scared it was going to be too hard for them. So she came in as a cowboy character named Howdy Dowdy and shared with them in a humorous way all about multiplication. "I have two cousins, Addeee and Multiii. Now when Addeee adds numbers up she gets tired, but with Multiii it's like going from walking to flying!" Then she showed them physically with manipulatives what multiplication is, and the next day they did a work sheet.

Nicknamed "Sparky" by her college speech class, Judy always tries to have the students apply what they're learning to the world around them. They did countless science experiments and went on field trips often. On one such outing, she took fifty children to the Aerospace Academy at the University of Oklahoma, where they made and shot off rockets, and created and used telescopes.

When they did addition and subtraction, she computer-simulated a class trip to the Six Flags over Texas amusement park. They figured the cost on the board and then compared it to the cost for their individual family to go. Her "open" classroom tended to have more activity and she allowed more physical movement, which was great for her Doer/Mover students. But the buzzing noise level —although under control—can be distracting to some kids.

working with the teacher

How can children's different learning needs be met and strengths built on in a classroom with over twenty children? If you or I had twenty-five children at home, we couldn't instruct each individually any more than a teacher could in a classroom.

With forty-five-minute classes in the normal middle school—fifteen of which are taken up with taking attendance, paperwork, and settling kids down—and trying to teach children with a broad range of abilities and developmental stages, teachers have their hands full. That's why I feel learning-style information is most helpful to parents and students. Although you can't completely change the teacher's style any more than you can change the child's learning style, you can:

- Make the teacher aware of the child's learning style, but don't expect her to change the class instruction and procedure just for your child.

- Ask for modifications that will help your child succeed and learn. It is especially important to find a strategy to bypass or manage a weakness that intrudes on your child's productivity, hinders achievement, or reduces his self-concept.

- Teach your child to adapt and compensate.

- Show your child how to change the information, whenever possible, into a form that his brain best comprehends and remembers.

Here are some ways to work with teachers—without alienating them—when modifications for a child's learning style need to be made:

Start at the beginning of the school year. Try to head off any problems before the child starts failing or becomes so frustrated that she acts out and her behavior deteriorates. The purpose is not to share negative information, but to open up communication.

Have a conference with the teacher. You could say, "This is what we've seen in the past and what we're working on. Sometimes Matt has a hard time focusing in on the instruction and dealing with distractions if he's in the back of the room. Could you seat him close to the front? We'd very much appreciate it. And if there's a problem, please let us know right away."

Children don't have to be certified "learning disabled" to have modifications made in the classroom. In fact, it can be better not to have them given a negative label if support can be provided and small modifications made. Usually, if teachers are approached graciously, they will make modifications. They want the child to succeed too. (Even if a student is learning disabled and has an Individualized Education Plan [IEP], parents need to check with the school periodically and make sure the support is being provided and the provisions for the student are being carried out. Don't assume everything is taken care of. No one can be your child's advocate for the long term but you.) In the process, don't make excuses for the child or take over his homework responsibilities.

As Marilyn Morgan, a veteran teacher, says, "Don't handicap your child by making excuses for him or by telling him, 'You can't do this.' We have many students today who have had excuses made for them and haven't learned to compensate and put out effort to overcome their obstacles or use their strengths in the regular classroom. Parents often take all the responsibility for learning away from the child."

Be careful that when you ask for a change, it is to empower and equip your child, to bypass a weakness and thus help your child succeed, not to take responsibilities or challenges away from her. The student needs to show initiative and make the effort to compensate and learn. We can encourage her to show interest by coming in for extra help when needed and asking the teacher for help when she doesn't understand something. If she gets an extra week to work on a report because of handwriting problems or slow reading skills, she can "repay" the accommodation by making a poster or video clip to accompany it.[3]

If you volunteer in the classroom, you'll find new ways to support your child's homework and study. In addition, the teacher is usually more open to your input and suggestions. Kathy, a mother of four boys, two of whom have some learning problems, found helping in her sons' classes one of the most valuable things she did during their elementary years. She learned what the expectations and homework requirements were like; she saw ways she could assist them at home, and her relationship with the teacher grew. "Besides, I love being a part of their world," said Kathy. When you volunteer and see what's going on in the classroom, you can head off problems before they become serious.

making modifications — overcoming weaknesses

When your child has a weakness that is hindering learning, many possibilities can remedy the situation. What we need to keep in mind is: Are we setting the student up for success or for failure? Very observant teachers may intuitively adapt lessons, or they may need the suggestions of parents, tutors, or the student himself. If we know where a student is apt to encounter difficulties, we can help him deal with it and avoid a breakdown in learning.

Here are some other modifications that can be made to facilitate students' learning, to manage and compensate for weaknesses, and to build on strengths:

A laptop computer in the classroom. All students need keyboarding skills, but especially those who have difficulty with handwriting or the output of information. If a student's fine motor skills are not developed enough to permit fast, neat penmanship, or if a student is very tactile and kinesthetic, or has some memory problems, a computer in class is a lifesaving tool for writing reports and recording class notes. As Dr. Mel Levine says, "A word processor is like an extra memory. Kids who have some memory problems might find that a word processor really improves their ability to write."[4] Of course, you'll need to get the approval of the teacher and the school before sending a laptop to school.

Modifying for movement. Kinesthetic learners who have a need for movement and for whom "sitting still" can take all their concentration can be helped by having two desks. One teacher shared with me that for one of her students, this modification made a terrific improvement in behavior and focus. When the student began to lose concentration, she could move to the other chair, quietly, not disturbing others. The teacher also had her pass out papers and tests and deliver notes to the office, which gave her further opportunities to move (and help at the same time).

Rocking, pedaling, and reading. Innovative teachers have provided beanbag chairs and a big rug in a comfortable "reading center," a rocking chair to read in (the rocking movement helps some students concentrate), or a stationary bike with a stand to hold a book, in which a student can pedal and read. One teacher who allowed his reading-troubled "movers" to pedal and read found it made a big difference in comprehension and interest. J. C., one of the students, said, "When I got up there, when I started to read, it was like a miracle. I started laughing because I couldn't help it, because I was reading almost one-hundred percent better."[5]

Class seating. For easily distracted students, or students whose concentration seems to wander when they sit in the back, sitting close to the front of the room can help them concentrate. Visual learners also do better when seated close to the front. Auditory students who are distracted by sounds and have trouble filtering out noise when trying to concentrate can be seated where they can hear without being distracted (for example, by the door where people are passing in the hall would not be an ideal place). A student who needs silence to help her concentrate in the classroom can be aided by earphones or earplugs.

Visual aids. If the teacher lectures a lot, a graphic accompaniment should be provided for a visual learner, especially if auditory processing is weak or delayed. Either an outline on the board or a partially blank copy of the teacher's outline for the student to take notes on and fill in, greatly aids learning. Using visual methods like mind mapping (or webbing, clustering) on the board or overhead transparencies, diagrams, and charts will also benefit students with a weak visual memory.

Tape recorder. Brad is a bright auditory learner in the sixth grade who has trouble taking class notes and following directions due to some delay in fine motor-skills development. He takes a small tape recorder to every class and records teacher presentations and instructions for assignments and then reviews these at home before doing his homework. He also has two of his textbooks on tape to listen to as he reads. Students whose reading level is deficient can qualify for books on tape through the Library of Congress and get novels and textbooks on tape to aid their learning. For a student who needs to hear test questions in addition to seeing them, the test can be read aloud or tape-recorded, with the student writing the answers on the test paper or providing them on tape.

Class discussions. Some students "freeze up" when randomly called on in class to answer questions. They may know the information, but when put on the spot they experience anxiety or can't think of the words fast enough. This kind of problem can be greatly helped with some communication and an agreement between teacher and student. For Mary, that meant the teacher didn't call on her unless her hand was up to volunteer an answer. Another teacher agreed to not call on a student until she was standing in front of her desk to "cue" her. In another classroom, the agreement was that the teacher would call on Beau only for questions that could be answered with yes or no for the first few weeks of school.

Timed tests. Some students find that the pressure of timed tests causes such anxiety that they forget all they studied and knew of the material. Others just need more time to get their ideas down on paper. Allowing extra time on tests or for written assignments can greatly help these students.

Varying teaching styles. If you are a homeschool mom or a classroom teacher and are introducing a new concept, such as the reproductive parts of a flower and how that connects to genetics, you can teach to a different style each day. The first day introduce the subject to your kids in a hands-on way (dissecting the flowers on white paper and identifying the parts); the next day help your children draw diagrams of the flower and label the parts (visual and kinesthetic); and the next day, devote some time to reading aloud and discussing the science book. Then have kids make clusters on big butcher paper of everything they've learned about flowers (auditory and visual).

Allow different forms of evaluation and "products" or results, which will be evaluated for a grade. For example, in lieu of a written composition on a chapter of science or history, a kinesthetic student could choose to produce a diorama; devise and set up an experiment; or make a learning center, relief map, educational game, or mobile. A visual student could elect to make a poster, produce a video or create a time line or advertising brochure for the class. An auditory student could produce and record a radio commentary; make an oral presentation to the class; or write a newspaper article, journal entry, or speech. Three kids could combine talents and produce a documentary on a subject. They can use a computer to take a simulated space trip, figure speed, do mathematical calculations, and record the results of their space journey to print out.

While providing a bypass strategy, we also help kids understand how they learn, what their strengths and weaknesses are, and keep helping them work on the problem. Dr. Mel Levine suggests, for example, that a child who still doesn't know his math facts automatically in seventh grade may get extra time on speed drills in class but continues to work on these on the computer for ten minutes each night before bedtime. A student who forgets things she's studied for tests is taught memorizing strategies. A child with poor reading skills gets tutoring and drill on language sounds using alphabetic phonics methods or other ways.[6]

Whether it's providing a calculator or something as small as manipulatives to help in math class, earphones to drown out noise, or a stationary bike to ride while reading, when we support our kids, address their learning needs, and help them manage and compensate for their weaknesses, we can make a big difference in their motivation, reduce their frustration level, and most of all, raise achievement.

learning-different
people who achieved

When John Sabolich was in grade school, teachers wanted to flunk him out of every grade. But each year his mom pleaded with teachers to pass her son and each year he became more and more afraid of learning. In fourth, fifth, and sixth grades, John hid in the bathroom during tests. He felt like a dunce in the classroom and a reject on the playground—being the last to be chosen for teams at recess or PE class. Reading was a struggle for John. He could figure out a few words, but not well enough or fast enough to pass.

Instead, he drew pictures of rocket ships, flying saucers, and planes, and invented steam engines and spacecraft. His hero was Leonardo da Vinci. While everyone was taking a test, he daydreamed and doodled on paper how the latest rocket or airplane could work. After school he mixed up rocket fuel and tried to build the machines he designed and get them to fly. He also went to his dad's prosthetics office (where artificial limbs are made and fitted for amputees) and watched him help kids walk again. John was intrigued by his dad's tools and creative work, and he liked the fact that there was no written work to do. He decided he wanted to help amputees walk as his dad did.

In seventh grade, John brought his report card home with seven Fs. His dad came unglued that night; he ranted and railed and said John wouldn't amount to anything. John still remembers that traumatic night, crying about his failure until sunrise. He decided that night that no matter what, he would show everybody in the world he could achieve.

He envisioned himself in a race car at the back of the pack, and he had to catch up and win. John started staying up until 2:00 AM to get homework done. It took him a long time to do everything, but he was determined to catch up. He got his own tutor to help him learn and pass the next courses. A patient retired teacher, she helped him in reading and math and other subjects.

After constant work, John brought his grades up to Cs, then to Bs the next year. Then finally, with tremendous effort, in late high school he got straight As. He also began working for his father at age thirteen.

By graduation, John's goal was to study prosthetics and orthotics at New York University; he was first in his class. From his hard work in high school, he had taught himself the most efficient ways to study: underlining and highlighting important areas, skimming pages for main ideas, and learning how to take quick notes and zero in on what the professor was saying. John was strong in remembering diagrams and pictures, not words. "If you drew me a picture I could understand it, but just words left me cold," said John. Realizing his strengths, he was able to increase his ability to learn abstractly. And his dexterity in his hands, as well as creative problem-solving ability, boosted his engineering and design skill.

The man who almost flunked out of elementary school became the world's most famous inventor of specialized, high-tech prostheses like the "Oklahoma City Running Leg"; the "Sabolich Foot," made of elastic futuristic materials that absorb vertical shock and convert it to energy; and a bionic myoelectric arm that doctors call a technological wonder.

Because of John's determination, innovation, and technical ability, amputees all over the world are jumping for joy, dancing, cheerleading, running in races, skydiving, and living normal lives again. He even designed a unique sense-of-feel system to provide patients "feeling" in their artificial feet. Though he had trouble reading books as a kid, Sabolich authored his own book, *You're Not Alone,* the personal stories of thirty-eight amputees who faced the physical challenges of amputation and found the courage to go on with their lives.

learning differences and gifts

Is John Sabolich's strong three-dimensional thinking ability and visual-spatial style of learning a disability or a difference? Like Sabolich, there are many famous people who had learning differences that caused them struggles in school, and yet out of these differences emerged the very talents, skills, and intelligence that enabled them to make a great impact on their community and world.

Sir Winston Churchill had problems in reading, suffered from a speech defect, and was hyperactive as a child. He was placed in the lowest group, where the slow boys were taught English.[1] Yet Churchill, prime minister of England during World War II, became the moral leader of the free world, a heroic statesman, and a Nobel Prize winner. Louis Pasteur failed the entrance exams to medical school and was known as a hardworking plodder. A great scientist in adulthood, he discovered diseases spread by bacteria, which saved millions of lives. Thomas Edison had severe memory problems and said of school, "I remember that I was never able to get along at school. I was always at the foot of the class. I used to feel that the teachers did not sympathize with me, and that my father thought I was stupid."[2] But this great inventor developed electrical lighting, the phonograph, and many other inventions. Woodrow Wilson, who did not learn the letters of the alphabet until he was nine, became the twenty-seventh president of the United States.[3]

Whether they had bad handwriting, trouble with spelling, or difficulty with abstract math concepts, or reading, these leaders found ways to bypass or compensate for their weaknesses. What mattered most for each of them was focusing and capitalizing on their strengths, developing a vision and hope for the future, and applying the determination and perseverance to do what it took to reach their goals. Not all of the people in my learning-different hall of fame have become world famous, but all have made significant contributions. That's why I encourage you to read this chapter aloud to your kids and especially those who have any learning challenges.

Meet Fred Epstein, who wasn't a good student in his early school years. His grades in college were only average, and in chemistry they were dismal. Yet he was determined to become a doctor. After being turned down by four medical schools, he was admitted to New York Medical College and became a pediatric neurosurgeon who has made a career of doing what medicine said could not be done: operating on and removing lethal tumors from the tiny brain stems of children.[4]

Epstein took on cases that other neurosurgeons wouldn't touch. His willingness to take calculated risks, his fierce determination, his incredible technical skill, and his refusal to accept defeat enabled him to move neurosurgery to frontiers thought impossible a decade ago and in the process save the lives of countless children.[5]

When Bodie Thoene, an award-winning author, was in the third grade, she already felt like a failure. As she tried to figure out how she could break the news to her parents, she stared at her report card.

"Math: C . . . not so bad. Spelling: F . . . disaster. Reading: F . . . major disaster. Conduct: C . . . oh, well. Effort: E . . . my life was over," Bodie said. The teacher had called her lazy. Another student had called her stupid. "Could I be both of those terrible things? It was the blackest day of my eight-year-old life, for I knew I had disappointed my parents. Mama called me bright. Daddy called me his little 'go-getter.' Didn't this report card repudiate everything they believed about me?"[6]

Her parents kept believing in her talents, and that summer

they found an enthusiastic tutor who helped her learn to read and write. From third grade on, her dream was to be a professional writer. School continued to be a struggle and high school was the most difficult experience of her life, except for a teacher who encouraged her creative writing. In spite of her Ds in English (because of mechanics), Mrs. Gaede saw Bodie's incredible grasp of language. But math was a foreign concept, and it nearly kept her from graduating from high school. She had spelling problems and trouble in reading.

Yet with her sharp auditory skills, Bodie's ability to hear dialogue and write the way real people think and talk enabled her to become one of the youngest successful scriptwriters in Hollywood—for John Wayne movies. A picture-visual learner, Bodie told such convincing tall tales as a child that people believed them to be true. Her great imagination enables her to "see" in her mind's eye the scenes in the award-winning historical fiction novels she and her husband, Brock, coauthor. Brock does the research and compiles the facts, and Bodie makes it entertainment.

what can we learn

What can we learn from the stories of these people who learned so differently but achieved so much? In all these people, their drive and determination go back to their difficult times as children. Although they had big obstacles to overcome, those very challenges were what propelled them to set goals, understand their strengths and weaknesses, find strategies to overcome the barriers, and achieve. Each had weaknesses, but strengths and gifts as well.

There was another striking similarity: Someone came alongside to give assistance, tutoring, and encouragement, and to see the positives instead of focusing on the negatives or failures. For Bodie Thoene, it was her parents who believed in her gifts and the teacher who tutored her in reading all summer, who realized she couldn't learn with phonics and used another method to teach her. For John Sabolich, it was a tutor who helped him fill in the gaps and learn how to study, and his vision for the bright future he could have pursuing the field of prosthetics like his dad as he worked side by side with him in his clinic.

Whether it was a parent, relative, teacher, or tutor who acted as mentor, they made all the difference. If you have a learning-different child, you too can make a world of difference in her life.

whatever the child's strengths

Focus on the positives rather than the negatives. Whether your child likes to paint abstract watercolors, tinker with computers, play the drums, write stories, or fix lawnmowers, accept and highlight those unique strengths, even if they are not your interests. We may not prize a certain skill or possess it ourselves, but if we nurture the seed of a talent in our child today, in years to come, with practice and hard work, it may develop into a fulfilling hobby or even career. Avoid equating success with only school-related/ academic pursuits. For some young people, especially high-energy Doers or spatially talented people, "blooming in life may have more to do with achieving success in artistic, mechanical, or athletic areas."[7]

Respect individuality in your family. Your child may not have the sports ability of the rest of your family, but prefers art. Or he may not have the "math smarts" his siblings do, but is mechanically or spatially talented. One child may be a real talker in the midst of quiet family members or sing all the time when nobody else can carry a tune. Celebrate the differences! When uniqueness is respected in a family, it frees each member to develop his own personality and special talents and capitalize on his learning strengths.

Be aware that as your child grows, new skills and talents will develop. Kids' minds are amazing and something they don't know at age ten can click and make sense six months later. They are always developing and growing in new ways. So be filled with hope as you watch your kids' learning and future unfold and share that hope with them.

Show your child you value his work, even early attempts. Have a special frame to hang the newest painting, or designate a wall in the house for a gallery of his framed drawings and paintings. Send off your budding writer's best poems to a children's magazine, and enter science projects in school science fairs and young inventors' exhibits and contests. Encourage entrepreneurial efforts if your child shows business savvy and wants to try out ideas for making money.

Don't criticize or squelch your child's enthusiasm. Refrain from comments like, "You aren't playing that piece on the piano again!" or "What's that?" when looking at your child's abstract watercolor painting. Rather, support your child's endeavors. Just a few words of encouragement are powerful motivators for your child's developing talent.

Luciano Pavarotti, the great opera singer, tells what his family's encouragement meant to his career as a world-famous opera singer. As a young boy, his grandmother put him on her lap while he hummed an Italian nursery rhyme and said, "You're going to be great, you'll see." He was a poor student in school, but his mother dreamed he'd be a successful banker. Instead, he taught elementary school and sang infrequently. "But my father constantly goaded me, saying I was singing below my potential," Pavarotti said. Finally, at age twenty-two, he quit teaching and started selling insurance to provide time and money to develop his vocal talent. He says studying voice with an outstanding teacher was the turning point of his life. "It's a mistake to take the safe path in life. If I hadn't listened to my father and dropped teaching, I would never be here. And yes, my teacher groomed me. But no teacher ever told me I would become famous. Just my grandmother."[8]

Help your child learn to deal with failure and bounce back without being devastated. When an experiment or project doesn't work, saying, "It's okay, because scientists fail their way to success" motivates lots more than, "I told you it wouldn't work." You can point out that Jonas Salk failed countless times before finding a polio vaccine that stopped a worldwide epidemic, and that Edison failed hundreds of times before he developed the lightbulb. Whether it's a musical tryout your child failed, a team he didn't make, or a science fair she didn't win, let him know your love isn't conditional upon his performance. Help him look at the failures or setbacks and say, "What can I learn from this?" and go on. Be prepared to accept incomplete projects and even a change of direction as your child finds what to try next time.

Talk to teachers about your child's strengths and how these could be maximized at school. Carrie shared with her son Noah's teacher at the first of the year that he loved to work and carry responsibility. So the teacher gave Noah the job of being computer lab monitor. Every morning he came early to uncover and turn on the computers. Each afternoon after school, he cleaned up the lab, turned off, and covered all the computers. Noah never missed a day the entire year and was so responsible they put two students under his supervision in the computer lab. He had some other academic challenges he was working on in the classroom, but recognizing and developing one of his strengths at school built his confidence and self-esteem.

Provide a support system. All of us have weaknesses and need support of some kind—a calculator to speed up math computation, a tutor to teach some new study strategies, glasses or contacts to improve weak vision, or a computer with spell-check capacity to compose written reports. Stephen Cannell is a successful, creative television writer and producer who has produced over two dozen prime-time series. His talent is writing, but his weakness in reading causes him to transpose numbers and letters and have trouble with spelling and sequencing. Instead of spending his time trying to correct the problems that have plagued him since childhood, he dictates scripts for his assistant or types them on computer and has an assistant proofread and polish the rough places.[9]

Keep believing. Find out what help your child needs, what strategies it will take to bypass weaknesses, and provide that support. And no matter how your children are doing right now, no matter what problems or struggles they are experiencing, keep believing in your kids, have high hopes and realistic expectations they can meet, and they'll grow in confidence and motivation. Their motivation is fueled by our hope and belief in them—that they do have strengths and gifts, and that with hard work and persistence, they will bloom. Although they may be developing slower physically or intellectually, or may learn differently from other students, they have talents and are full of promise.

Jim Trelease tells of his brother Brian, who was always in remedial reading classes. Of four boys in their family, he took the longest to graduate from college, but was the only one to graduate with honors and the only one who got a master's degree. He is also the only one of the brothers to become a CEO of a major corporation. He tells how his father, who must have sensed Brian had some spark of business savvy, read the *Wall Street Journal* every night to him, while upstairs Jim thought—how silly—he doesn't even understand it and couldn't read it himself. Now Brian's corporation runs ads in the *Wall Street Journal.*[10]

We are tempted to write many kids off academically. But let me encourage you not to write them off—not to let a teacher write them off—and not ever to give up on them. Instead, show them how to capitalize on their learning-style strengths and develop their gifts. Keep believing in them and providing the verbal, physical, emotional, and spiritual support they need to succeed. Even with tremendous obstacles, if kids are believed in and encouraged, they can accomplish amazing things.

notes

chapter 1: no two children learn alike

1. Carol Marshall and Kaye Johns, *Success Strategies for At-Risk Students: Center for Success in Learning Manual* (Dallas: Center for Success in Learning, 1992), p. 3.
2. Linda Verlee Williams, *Teaching for the Two-Sided Mind: A Guide to Right Brain/Left Brain Education* (New York: Simon & Schuster, 1986), p. 145.
3. Sometimes educational and/or diagnostic testing is needed to determine the causes and range of a child's school-related problems. School psychometricians can assess a child's abilities, and the local university's learning centers and education professors or developmental specialists are excellent sources of diagnostic testing and professional evaluation.
4. *Center for Success in Learning News*, volume 6, number 1 (October/November 1991).

chapter 2: identifying your child's learning style

1. Quoted in Susan Lapinski, "Learning Disabilities: Mastering the Challenge," *Child Magazine* (December/January 1992), p. 74.

chapter 3: discovering your own learning style

1. Carol Marshall and Kaye Johns, *Success Strategies for At-Risk Students: Center for Success in Learning Manual* (Dallas: Center for Success in Learning, 1992), p. 3:4.

chapter 4: talkers and listeners

1. Karen DeClouet, *Teaching Children to Teach Themselves* (Iberia, LA: Success in School, 1992), p. 10.

2. Rita Dunn, quoted in Carol Marshall and Kaye Johns, *Success Strategies for At-Risk Students: Center for Success in Learning Manual* (Dallas: Center for Success in Learning, 1992), p. 3:10.

3. Linda Verlee Williams, *Teaching for the Two-Sided Mind: A Guide to Right Brain/Left Brain Education* (New York: Simon & Schuster, 1983), p. 163.

4. Wanda Draper, *High Expectations,* rev. ed. (Oklahoma City: Omni Productions, 1993), p. 2.

5. Draper, p. 2.

6. Williams, p. 31.

7. Carol McGehe, "Mathematics the Write Way," *Instructor Magazine* (April 1991), pp. 36–38.

chapter 5: doers and touchers

1. Elaine Gaines, *Math Alive* (Hot Sulphur Springs, CO: Educational Strategies for Mathematical Competency, 1993), pp. 5–6.

2. Priscilla Vail, *Learning Styles: Food for Thoughts and 130 Practical Tips for Teachers K–4* (Rosemont, NJ: Modern Learning Press, 1992), p. 13.

3. Gaines, p. 6.

4. Benjamin Spock, "The Best Way to Teach," *Parenting Magazine* (September 1993), pp. 113–116.

5. Ellen Hawkes, "I Had to Grow Up Fast," *Parade Magazine* (January 8, 1989), pp. 10–12.

6. Carol Marshall and Kaye Johns, *Success Strategies for At-Risk Students: Center for Success in Learning Manual* (Dallas: Center for Success in Learning, 1992), p. 3:26.

chapter 6: watchers

1. Karen DeClouet, *Teaching Children to Teach Themselves* (New Iberia, LA: Success in School, 1992), p. 29.

2. My thanks to Karen DeLouet for her collaboration on the Recall Note-Taking System and note-taking ideas.

3. Margie Golick, *Deal Me In! The Use of Playing Cards in Teaching and Learning* (NY: Monarch Press, 1981), pp. 20–22.

chapter 7: how learning styles impact reading skills

1. Rita Dunn, "A Research-based Plan for Students Doing Homework," *Early Years,* Volume 15 (December 1984), pp. 45–54.
2. Analysis of reading methods is adapted from consultations with reading specialists Karen Gale, Tim Campbell, Karen DeClouet, and the resources *Diagnostic Teaching of Reading: Techniques for Instruction and Assessment,* 2nd ed. and *Success Strategies for At-Risk Students: Center for Success in Learning Manual.*
3. For information on Parents Sharing Books, contact the Family Literacy Center of Indiana University, 1-800-759-4723.

chapter 8: discovering your child's talents and gifts

1. Robert Sternberg, "Second Game: The School's Eye View of Intelligence," in *Language, Literacy, and Culture: Issues of Society and Schooling,* ed. J.A. Langer (Norwood, NJ: Ablex, 1987), pp. 25–29, 23–78.
2. Sternberg, p. 25.
3. Sternberg, p. 25.
4. Robert J. Trotter, "Three Heads Are Better Than One," *Psychology Today* (August 1986), pp. 56–62.
5. Donald Clifton and Paula Nelson, *Soar with Your Strengths* (New York: Delacorte Press, 1992), p. 72.
6. Dr. Mel Levine, *Keeping a Head in School: A Student's Book About Learning Abilities and Learning Disorders* (Toronto: Educators Publishing Service, 1990), p. 283.
7. Howard Gardner, *Multiple Intelligences: The Theory in Practice* (New York: Basic Books, 1993), p. 27.

chapter 9: developing your child's talents and gifts

1. Victor Goertzel and Mildred Goertzel, *Cradles of Eminence: A Provocative Study of the Childhoods of over 400 Famous Twentieth-Century Men and Women* (Boston: Little, Brown, 1962), p. xii.
2. Robert Sternberg, as quoted in Robert J. Trotter, "Three Heads Are Better Than One," *Psychology Today* (August 1986), p. 59.
3. Sternberg in Trotter, p. 59.

4. Howard Gardner, *Frames of Mind* (New York: Basic Books, 1993), p. 162.
5. Robert Sternberg, "Second Game: The School's Eye View of Intelligence," in *Language, Literacy, and Culture: Issues of Society and Schooling,* ed. J.A. Langer (Norwood, NJ: Ablex, 1987), pp. 27–28.
6. Gardner, *Frames of Mind,* p. 181.
7. Donald Clifton and Paula Nelson, *Soar with Your Strengths* (New York: Delacorte Press, 1992), p. 60.

chapter 10: handling weaknesses so they don't block strengths

1. Dr. Mel Levine, *A Mind at a Time* (New York: Simon & Schuster, 2002), p. 281.
2. Levine, *A Mind at a Time,* p. 281.
3. Levine, *A Mind at a Time,* p. 281.
4. Mel Levine, *Keeping a Head in School* (Toronto: Educators Publishing Service, 1990), p. 270.
5. Marlene LeFever, "How Our Children Learn," *Today's Better Life* (Winter 1992), p. 45.
6. Levine, *A Mind at a Time,* p. 282.

chapter 11: learning-different people who achieved

1. Victor Goertzel and Mildred Goertzel, *Cradles of Eminence: A Provocative Study of the Childhoods of over 400 Famous Twentieth-Century Men and Women* (Boston: Little, Brown, 1962), p. 265.
2. Goertzel and Goertzel, p. 248.
3. Goertzel and Goertzel, p. 5.
4. Fred J. Epstein with Elaine Shimberg, "I Don't Accept Children Dying," *Reader's Digest* (February 1993), p. 201.
5. Epstein and Shimberg, p. 202.
6. Bodie and Brock Thoene, *Writer to Writer* (Minneapolis: Bethany, 1990), pp. 39–41.
7. Thomas Armstrong, *In Their Own Way* (Los Angeles: Tarcher, 1987), p. 141.
8. Glenn Plaskin, *Turning Point: Pivotal Moments in the Lives of America's Celebrities* (New York: Carol Publishing, 1992), p. 178.

9. Donald Clifton and Paula Nelson, *Soar with Your Strengths* (New York: Delacorte Press, 1992), pp. 76–77.
10. Jim Trelease, "Turning On the Turned Off Reader," audiotape (Springfield, Mass.: Reading Tree Productions).

recommended books

Armstrong, Thomas. *In Their Own Way: Discovering and Encouraging Your Child's Multiple Intelligences.* Los Angeles: Tarcher, 1987.

Armstrong, Thomas. *The Multiple Intelligences of Reading and Writing: Making the Words Come Alive.* Alexandria, VA: Association for Supervision and Curriculum Development, 2003.

Bradway, Lauren, and Barbara Hill. *How to Maximize Your Child's Learning Ability.* Garden City, NY: Avery Publishing, 1993.

Campbell, Ross. *How to Really Love Your Child.* Colorado Springs, CO: Cook Communications, 2004.

Fuller, Cheri. *How to Grow a Young Music Lover.* Colorado Springs, CO: Waterbrook/Shaw, 2002.

Fuller, Cheri. *Opening Your Child's Nine Learning Windows.* Grand Rapids, MI: Zondervan, 2001.

Gardner, Howard. *Intelligence Reframed.* New York: Basic Books/ Perseus Book Group, 1999.

Gardner, Howard. *The Disciplined Mind: Beyond Facts and Standardized Tests, the K-12 Education That Every Child Deserves.* New York: Simon & Schuster, 1999.

Healy, Jane. *Endangered Minds: Why Children Don't Think and What We Can Do About It.* New York: Simon & Schuster, 1990.

Healy, Jane. *Failure to Connect: How Computers Affect Our Children's Minds.* New York: Simon & Schuster, 1998.

Levine, Mel, M.D. *A Mind at a Time.* New York: Simon & Schuster, 2002.

Tobias, Cynthia Ulrich. *The Way They Learn.* Colorado Springs, CO: Focus on the Family, 1994.

Vail, Priscilla L. *Liberate Your Child's Learning Patterns.* New York: Kaplan, 2004.

Vail, Priscilla. *Seize the Meaning! Help Your Child Move from Learning to Read to Reading to Learn.* New York: Kaplan, 2002.

about the author

Cheri Fuller is an award-winning author, a speaker, and an experienced educator who has taught every level from elementary to college. She is the author of thirty books including *Opening Your Child's Nine Learning Windows*, *Extraordinary Kids* (coauthored with Louise Tucker Jones), *How to Grow a Young Music Lover*, *When Mothers Pray*, and numerous articles in *Family Circle*, *Child*, *Parents of Teenagers*, *Focus on the Family*, and other publications. She's a guest on numerous television and radio programs each year and is a popular speaker at conferences, parent groups, and women's retreats both in the United States and internationally. She was named Oklahoma Mother of the Year for 2004. She and her husband, Holmes, live in Oklahoma and have three grown children.

To contact Cheri Fuller for speaking engagements or for her resources and materials, visit her website, www.cherifuller.com.

Other books in the SCHOOL SAVVY KIDS series by Cheri Fuller.

School Starts at Home

Discover how you can foster a stimulating, creative environment for your children by modeling a love of learning at home.
1-57683-600-2

Raising Motivated Kids

Packed with dozens of helpful hints, this book will show you how to turn your parental insight into powerful motivation to help your kids succeed in life.
1-57683-601-0

To get your copies, visit your local bookstore.